DISCOVERING THE CONTENTS OF A
Wounded & Broken
Heart

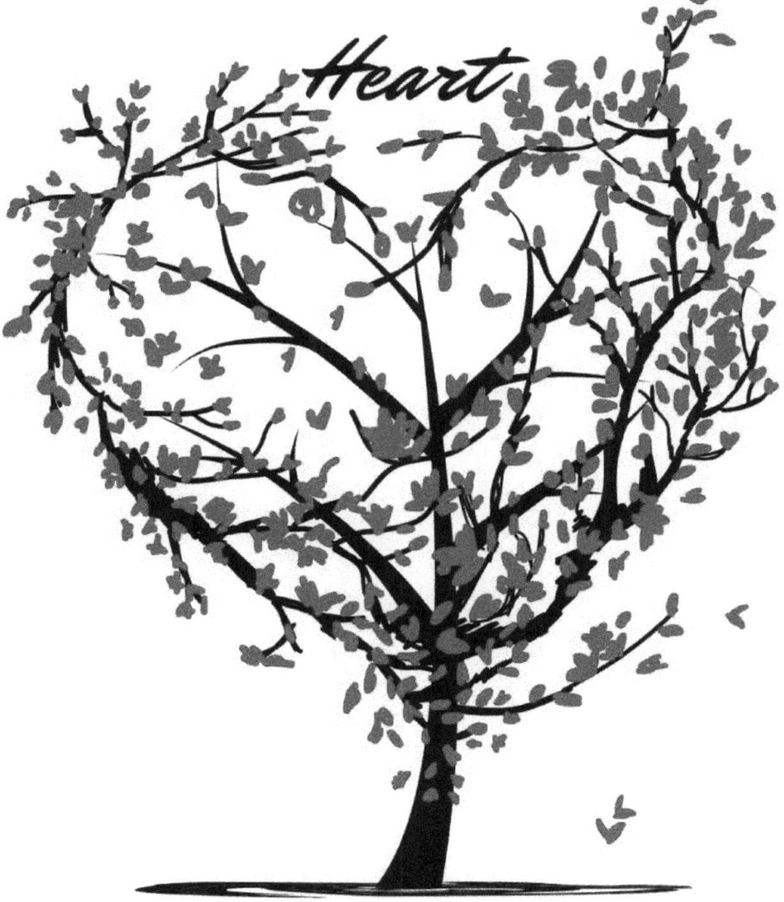

KAREN HYMON

©Copyright 2024-Karen Hymon

All rights reserved. This book is protected by the copyright laws of the United States of America. No part of this publication may be reproduced, distributed, stored in a retrieval system, or transmitted in any form or by any means, electronic, mechanical, photocopying, recording or otherwise, without the prior written permission of the copyright holder.

Unless otherwise indicated, all Scripture quotations are taken from the New King James Version of the Holy Bible. Other notable versions include King James Version and the New International Version.

For permission requests, write to the author at the address below.

KarenHymon@gmail.com

This book was edited, formatted, designed, and published by:

UNIQUE PUBLISHING HOUSE, LLC

P.O. Box 750792, Memphis, TN 38175

www.uniquehouse.org

Cover art by Mikala Symone Wheeler

ISBN: 979-8-9927463-2-7

DISCOVERING THE CONTENTS OF A
Wounded & Broken
Heart

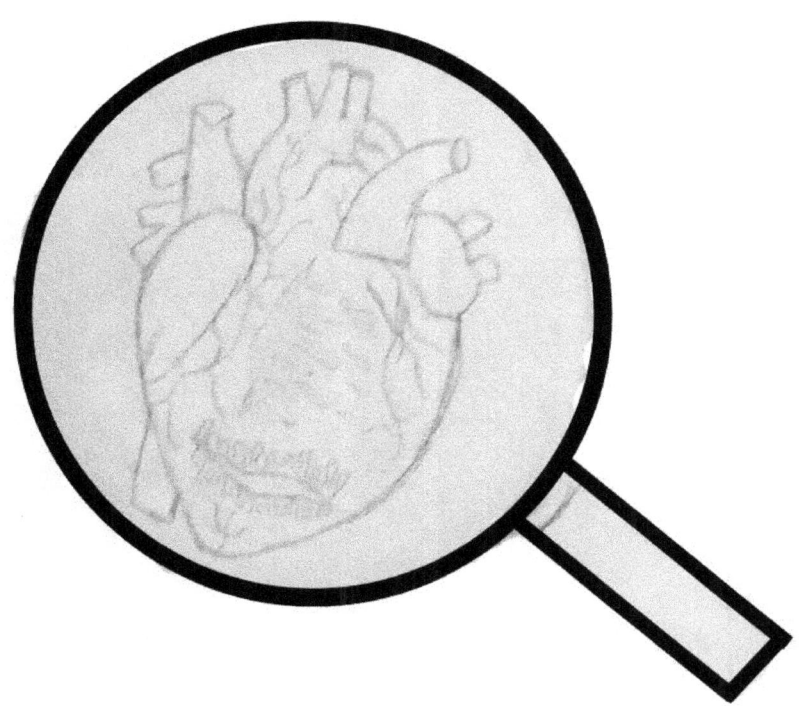

Dedication

This book is dedicated to all those who are truly longing after God's perfect will for their lives and desiring to know what lies hidden in the secret places of the heart. I pray that as you read this book, you too will discover the contents of your own heart and begin the journey to freedom.

Acknowledgments

I'm extremely grateful for the leading and teaching of my spiritual leaders, Apostle Tony Wade & Prophetess Felecia Wade. Under their guidance, I can truly say that what I have learned on this journey would not have been possible without their roles in my life as Good Shepherds. I would also like to give a shout out to Pastors Kevin & Shondra Baker for their encouragement and the chastising (I needed it!) Finally, to my little sister, Dr. Candace Jones, thank you for whipping me into shape.

Table of Contents

Reflection i
Introduction ii

Part 1: Emotions 1

    Fear 9
    Insecurity 18
    Rejection 25
    Offense 29
    Bitterness 38
    Pride 42
    Sexual Immorality 51

Part 2: Deliverance 72

    Wisdom 76
    Justice 89
    Holiness 84

Part 3: Righteousness/Sanctification 96

    Fruit of the Spirit 102
        Love 104
        Joy 107
        Peace 111
        Patience 115
        Faithfulness 119
        Longsuffering 124
        Goodness 128
        Meekness & Gentleness 132
        Self-Control 136

Reflection

When I look back over my life and the events (losses, the pain, the disappointments), I am reminded by these scriptures that I have a Father who loves me, an adversary who hates me and the responsibility to stand and fight for my life.

John 1:1(KJV) *In the beginning was the Word, and the Word was with God, and the Word was God. v.4 In Him was life, and the life was the light of men.*

Matthew 24:27(NKJV) *For as the lightning comes from the east and flashes to the west, so also will the coming of the Son of Man be.*

Jeremiah 29:11 (NKJV) *For I know the thoughts that I think toward you, says the Lord, thoughts of peace and not of evil, to give you a future and a hope.*

John 10:10 (NKJV) *The thief does not come except to steal, and to kill, and to destroy. I have come that they may have life, and that they may have it more abundantly.*

1 Timothy 5:24 AMPC *The sins of some men are conspicuous (openly evident to all eyes), going before them to the judgment [seat] and proclaiming their sentence in advance; but the sins of others appear later [following the offender to the bar of judgment and coming into view there]*

Introduction

The Bible says *"and they overcame him by the Blood of the Lamb and by the word of their testimony;* Revelation 12:11 (NKJV)." This is my testimony, one that I have lived for the past 48 years. My life is summed up in divisions; from birth to twelve years, thirteen years to forty-six years, and forty-six years and beyond. There's a simple explanation for the divisions. At twelve years old, I received salvation: I fell in love with the "idea" of God, Jesus & Holy Spirit, but had no true relationship with Him or Them. Don't get me wrong, as a youngster, I was fascinated with learning about Jesus and His salvation but never knew that salvation was only the beginning. In fact, I only received one half of the salvation package; no powerful gift of speaking in other tongues that would take my prayer life and walk to a whole new level; no sweet Holy Spirit to empower, comfort, lead and guide me into all truth. I didn't understand what "Sonship" meant, definitely had never heard of it and so from the ages of thirteen to forty-six, I lived a religious, legalistic, and crossless Christianity as a result of my undeveloped fellowship with the Father and lack of sound doctrine. This pseudo-life left me seeking something and never finding it, and practicing sin; which, in turn, left me broken and wounded. I remember at times being truly desperate for that "something" that I was missing but had no idea of what it was that I was seeking. Had the Lord turned His back on me, I too, like the rich man, would have been in hell "lifting up my eyes." My life was profoundly and irrevocably changed in September of 2016 at Divine Life Church, pastored by Apostle Tony and Pastor Felecia Carter Wade, located at 2019 Ball Road. There I met the living Savior and began the process of becoming the person whom God intended me to be.

The title of my book, *"Discovering the Contents of a Broken & Wounded Heart"* is pivotal because in order for me to be free and to embrace my destiny in the Lord, I had to understand what lay hidden in my heart and the source from which it arose. When the Lord became real to me in 2016, He took me on a whirlwind journey of self-discovery and of uncovering the issues of my heart. In fact, exactly 12 months after I joined this church, the Lord led me on a 28-day water only fast. How did I know it was the Lord? It is because the Bible says that in our flesh dwells no good thing. On my own, I'd never consider going one day without food, let alone 28 days. After completing the fast, I understood the purpose was to draw me closer to Him and to open my spiritual eyes to discern that I was broken beyond belief.

Why is it important to know what lies in our hearts? The Bible says in *1 Timothy 5:24 GNT The sins of some people are plain to see, and their sins go ahead of them to judgment; but the sins of others are seen only later.* This verse refers to the sin that lies hidden in our hearts, those secret things which only our Father can see. The Lord is the one who judges the heart, so it is better for me to learn the contents on my own with the help of Holy Spirit and to yield my brokenness to Him now, than to stand in judgment later.

Proverbs 4:23(NKJV) states, *"Keep your heart with all diligence, for out of it spring the issues of life."* This encompasses "the thought life, the emotions, the wellsprings of life." *"Keep your heart with all diligence"*, it's a simple yet profound statement that determines the very trajectory of our lives. Our hearts must be attended to daily and with intent. As a twelve-year-old, I had no clue that my heart "should" or even "could" be kept. My early years were riddled with seeds sown in ignorance, doubt, and fear. The roots and the trees and indeed orchards that developed from those seeds have plagued me most of my adult life by keeping me bound to sin and living in defeat.

I wrote this book because I came into the true knowledge of Christ rather late. I had zero knowledge of the supernatural and how what I said controlled my life. I knew that there would be others who, like me, were clueless and would require a guide to help them to uncover the wickedness of their hearts. As you read this book , please be prayerful about God leading you to uncover the hidden secrets in your heart. The book is broken up into the three main downfalls that we naturally struggle with; Emotions and the sins / pitfalls which often accompany skewed emotions, Deliverance and Righteousness and Sanctification. You will find as you seek God- these three areas will be key in determining your victory.

PART 1

Emotions

Emotions

Emotions. Emotional. Emoting. Feelings. Whichever way you look at the term, we are as human beings subject to them, oftentimes led by them, dominated by them, defined by them, ruled by them, and consumed with them. But what are they? Why do we have them? Where do they spring from? How are we to deal with them?

An emotion is a feeling such as happiness, love, fear, anger, or hatred, which can be caused by the situation that you are in or the people you are with.

Emotion is the part of a person's character that consists of their feelings, as opposed to their thoughts, (collinsdictionary.com).

Feelings: an emotion such as anger or happiness.

The following scriptures speak to our emotional state and the way that we should govern our souls. Remember, the soul is where our emotions reside. It is one of the reasons that our soul's salvation is a continuous process. God provided emotions as a way for us to show our pleasure and or displeasure with the world, the actions of others and ourselves. Since we are created in the image and likeness of God, it stands to reason that He made us as He is. He possesses all of the same emotions that we do. His character helps us to understand our own emotional responses as a healthy and whole individual. We learn that our anger should be tempered with mercy and our impatience with love, humility and longsuffering. We will discuss later on in depth how we are to deal with our emotions in a Godly manner.

Scriptural Truth

As you read this book, you will notice that there are several scriptures in each section. Holy Spirit wanted to include these so that there is a foundation for the reader to stand on and have a platform based on the Word to war with whatever issue that you are dealing with. We are to be washed with the Word. The scriptures give us comfort, reassurance, hope, correction, and victory.

Proverbs 16:32 KJV He that is slow to anger is better than the mighty; and he that ruleth his spirit than he that taketh a city

Philippians 4:7 KJV And the peace of God, which passeth all understanding, shall keep your hearts and minds through Christ Jesus.

1 Corinthians 14:32 KJV And the spirits of the prophets are subject to the prophets.

Colossians 3:2 KJV Set your affection on things above, not on things on the earth.

Romans 8:6 KJV For to be carnally minded is death; but to be spiritually minded is life and peace

Hebrews 11: 9-10 KJV By faith he sojourned in the land of promise, as in a strange country, dwelling in tabernacles with Isaac and Jacob, the heirs with him of the same promise: 10 For he looked for a city which hath foundations, whose builder and maker is God.

2 Corinthians 5:7 KJV (For we walk by faith, not by sight:)

Romans 1:17 KJV For therein is the righteousness of God revealed from faith to faith: as it is written, The just shall live by faith.

Psalms 139:23 KJV Search me, O God, and know my heart: try me, and know my thoughts

Proverbs 3:5-6 KJV Trust in the Lord with all thine heart; and lean not unto thine own understanding. In all thy ways acknowledge him, and he shall direct thy paths

Proper Emotional Response vs. Flawed/Improper Emotional Response

Truth must be the litmus test when dealing with our emotions. Truth refers to taking into account all of the relevant facts which pertain to a particular situation and then applying a (Godly) standard to ascertain the moral and righteous outcome. Truth is so important because our emotional state can make a mockery of the truth. Emotions are often one-sided and fueled by our perceptions of what we thought should or did happen. So now, the task is to look at our situations from the light of the Word of God; which will lead us directly to a proper emotional response.

Examples of a proper emotional response can be taken straight from scripture and further shows us the nature and the heart of our Father. In Genesis chapter 19, God's anger is poured out upon the wickedness of Sodom & Gomorrah and also on the Godless inhabitants of the earth during the time of Noah. It must be noted that God, even when faced with the utter wickedness taking place in Sodom & Gomorrah, showed mercy and restraint due to His relationship with His servant and friend Abraham. During that same time He demonstrates His love, mercy and compassion when He saves His servant Noah and family because of Noah's love, obedience and personal relationship with the Father. New Testament evidence proves that the Lord Jesus during His ministry years, showed exasperation with His disciples after coming down from the Mount of Transfiguration in Matthew 17. He was frustrated because of their inability to cast out the demon from the man's son. On another occasion, Jesus demonstrated His sorrow when

He wept for His friend Lazarus. Jesus was moved to compassion when He grieved with Mary, the sister of Lazarus. In Hebrews chapter 3: 9-11, God demonstrated remarkable long suffering as he dealt with the children of Israel (forty years of contending with their temptation of Him, their wicked hearts and their unwillingness to acknowledge His goodness and faithfulness) as He is leading them from the land of Egypt. His anger was kindled against them because of their sin and disregard for Him as the Great "I Am" and because of the consequences of their disregard, a generation's death ensued. As chronicled in each of the gospels, in some of the most moving passages of scripture, we see Jesus in the Garden of Gethsemane, praying in such anguish, that His sweat was like blood. This intense prayer was due to His impending passion and the subsequent separation from God, His Father for those three days of torment spent in Hell. During each of the above examples, we see the raw emotion that is exhibited, but in every instance the emotional response was held to a standard - the righteousness and holiness of God Himself.

Examples of a flawed or improper emotional response can be found in 1 Samuel 15 where we find the story of King Saul; who after disobeying God during the destruction of the Amalekites is called out on his disobedience. First, he blames the army and claims that the animals were to be sacrificed. Even after Samuel tells him what the Lord says, King Saul was more concerned with his reputation- and wanted to look good in front of the people. The posture of his heart was to do evil. The Bible says that out of the abundance of the heart the mouth speaks, Luke 6:45 paraphrase. So Saul's desire to please the people or to look good in front of the people superseded his desire to please God and to do His will. To sum it up, any emotional outbreak that leads to sin is improper. Be angry and sin not. Let us also look at King David, who allowed his lust for Bathsheba to lead him into a whirlwind of sin. However, when faced with the consequences of his actions, David referred back to the truth of God's Word and then recognized his error and showed true repentance and confessed his sin before God. Our unbridled dependence upon or reliance on our emotions can lead us into sin.

I can recall as I grew up, how my jacked up emotions ruled my life, especially around the time that I entered puberty. I can recall how I was easily offended and overly sensitive to the comments and actions of others. I spent so much time looking at the circumstances of my life and dwelling on what I perceived as the negatives until I could think of nothing else. I was an emotional wreck, spiraling into what I now know was depression, which I fueled by listening to depressing music that increased the melancholy. My emotional response was flawed to the point that I took on negative mindsets and attributes. The truth of my reality was lost to me as I looked at my own situation instead of looking unto Jesus.

During this time I was attempting to learn how to be a friend, and because of my flawed emotions and self-centered outlook, I was a terrible friend to many who meant well in my life. I was insecure, broken, and emotionally unavailable to extend compassion or feel true empathy. I did not cast down the thoughts that exalted themselves against God, instead, I believed the lies of the enemy lock, stock, and

barrel.

    I possessed no true compassion, and subsequently my words and actions were hurtful and damaging. I found myself caught in a web of petty jealousies that were projections of my own brokenness. Today, I find myself thinking of people who I need to apologize to and seek their forgiveness for my ugly words that were born out of my inability to see past my own hurt and disappointments. Holy Spirit is such a great revelator of what lies dormant in our hearts! I thank God for the Spirit of Truth and for His place in my life. I have literally not looked at these relationships from the lens of my own brokenness until now and have been able to see the part that I played in the demise of some relationships. I take this time to sincerely beg forgiveness of those that I hurt.

Make it PERSONAL

Emotional Intelligence is a relatively new term to me, but it makes so much sense when dealing with a broken heart. Understanding the true role of your emotions and how they should be a balanced component of your soul will aid you on your journey to discovering the contents of your heart. Emotions are crucial for our well-being but must be tempered by a strong foundation rooted in sonship and anchored by the truth of the word of God.

As you embark on this journey of self- discovery it is imperative to remember these points:

1. God made you.
2. You are fearfully and wonderfully made.
3. You were created in His image.

It is also important to ask yourself these questions:
1. Do my emotions own me?
2. Do I let my emotional state rule my entire day?
3. **Am I able to step back from a situation and view it rationally or are my feelings always in the forefront?**

Fear

Fear is a vicious root and a stronghold that the enemy attempts to use (often successfully) in a believer's life to keep them from reaching their God- given purpose and destiny. Let's be clear on this fact, Holy Spirit revealed that there is emotion, fear, and then there is the "Spirit of Fear". When one is experiencing the emotion of fear, it is usually a short-lived condition. However, when one is operating in the spirit of fear, things take a turn for the worse and then we see the devastation that the spirit of fear can cause in your life. The spirit of fear can be crippling and can cause instant stagnation resulting in cessation of forward progress towards goals, giftings, and callings. Fear is defined as (n.) an unpleasant emotion caused by the belief that someone or something is dangerous, likely to cause pain, or a threat; (v.) to be afraid of (someone or something) as likely to be dangerous, painful, or threatening. Fears manifest in many different forms, on a continuum from mild quirks to outright phobias such as racial discrimination and it often partners with hatred, another insidious tool of the enemy. The Bible is clear about fear and its place in a believers' life and heart. Holy Spirit led me to these scriptures where we find how the Father feels concerning fear and how we should handle that emotion. Fear is an emotion, and an important one, we should not shy away from feeling this because it can be essential to warn the believer of impending danger. The way that a believer reacts to fear should never be in the sense that we can be harmed, but in that a threat is present which must be confronted and defeated by the Word of God! The way in which we should react to fear is spelled out in the scriptures listed below. They are found in the Old Testament as well as under the New Covenant which reinforces the changelessness of our God and His stance on fear. As a matter of fact, He states that there should be one thing that you should fear in Matthew *10:28 (KJV) And fear not them which kill the body, but are not able to kill the soul: but rather fear* **him which is able to destroy both soul and body in hell.**

The following passages of scriptures provide reassurance as to how the Father loves and protects all of those who place their trust and hope in Him. They highlight one of our most enduring and sometimes misunderstood aspects of "who" we are in relationship to God the Father and that is our Sonship. Let's look at what the term means briefly.

Sonship: the understanding that the believer is a joint heir with Christ, His beloved, and is seated in heavenly places. It is also the understanding that Holy Spirit resides within us and is the dunamis power of God, and finally it is the understanding that as sons of God we have the power of authority imputed to us by Jesus Christ as part of the finished work of the cross over the enemy. In fact, when we recognize our position in God as His sons then there is no power in Hell that can stand against us!

The book of Isaiah leaves us with words of comfort and hope as the prophet proclaims what the Spirit of the Lord says to His people: *Isaiah 41:10 (KJV) Fear thou not; for I am with thee: be not dismayed; for I am thy God: I will strengthen thee; yea, I will help thee; yea, I will uphold thee with the right hand of my righteousness.* Our Father becomes even more personal as He speaks His love over our very lives; *Isaiah 43:1 (KJV paraphrased) But now thus saith the Lord that created thee, O Karen, and he that formed thee, O Karen, Fear not: for I have redeemed thee, I have called thee by thy name; thou art mine.*

Isaiah writes of my Creator, who became my Redeemer and Father the moment that I accepted His Son as my Savior. He reassures me that I belong to Him, and that indeed He knows my name and there is no reason to fear! I dare you to replace my name with your own and revel in His love for you!

Hebrews 13:6 (KJV) *So that we may boldly say, The Lord is my helper, and I will not fear what man shall do unto me.*

We are to operate in the spirit of boldness and confidence in who He is in and through us; unfailing and ever victorious!

John 14:27 (KJV) *Peace I leave with you, my peace I give unto you: not as the world giveth, give I unto you. Let not your heart be troubled, neither let it be afraid.*

The peace of our God will wrap us up and overwhelm us and is able to insulate us from the cares and trials of this world if only we will make our will subject to His perfect will for our lives!

1 John 4:18 (KJV) *There is no fear in love; but perfect love casteth out fear: because fear hath torment. He that feareth is not made perfect in love.*

John speaks of those who live in a constant state of fear as not being made "perfect" in love. How are we made perfect in love? We are made perfect by trusting that He has our lives firmly in His grasp and that He has a plan and a vision for us! Glory to God!

Deuteronomy 31:6-8 (KJV) *Be strong and of a good courage, fear not, nor be afraid of them: for the Lord thy God, he it is that doth go with thee; he will not fail thee, nor forsake thee. 7 And Moses called unto Joshua, and said unto him in the sight of all Israel, be strong and of a good courage: for thou must go with this people unto the land which the Lord hath sworn unto their fathers to give them; and thou shalt cause them to inherit it. 8 And the Lord, he it is that doth go before thee; he will be with thee, he will not fail thee, neither forsake thee: fear not, neither be dismayed.*

In the above passage, we are constantly reminded to be strong and to maintain courage in the knowledge of who it is who goes before us!

The God of all creation made Himself available to us and for us! That thought blows my mind! The King of Glory is on our side!! Hallelujah!!

Psalms 18:2 reveals to us more of the nature of our champion, He is a strong tower! Psalm 18:2 (KJV) *The Lord is my rock, and my fortress, and my deliverer; my God, my strength, in whom I will trust; my buckler, and the horn of my salvation, and my high tower.*

Having revealed His love and concern for us, and to us, now we can rest and do as 1 Peter 5:7 (KJV) says that we should do; 7 *Casting all your care upon him; for he careth for you.*

The Father understands our humanity and loves us so much that He still provides comfort to the broken by reminding us that the posture of our hearts should be to trust in Him. Psalm 56:3 (KJV) *What time I am afraid; I will trust in thee.*

Psalm 94:19 (CEV) *And when I was burdened with worries, you comforted me and made me feel secure.* The significance of this scripture is the Father saying to us that fear is real but it is canceled by trusting in Him. He is our security against anything or anyone that would attempt to come upon us to harm us. 2 Timothy 1:7(KJV) *For God hath not given us the spirit of fear; but of power, and of love, and of a sound mind.*

When I first received the mandate to write my story, I realized that fear was so much a part of me that I had no clue who I was. I had no identity and as such was tossed to and fro by the cares of life. Holy Spirit allowed me to recall a very important key which unlocked how fear entered my life. My earliest memories are surrounded by gut-wrenching fear and anxiety. These memories were of our coffee table in the living room of our home in Chicago. Each time that I recall it, the atmosphere in the room seems gloomy and cloudy as if there was something unclean and defiled present. I was probably about four or five years old at the time. It was a typical 1970's era table, rectangular, coffee brown in color, with two sliding doors in the middle for storage. I can remember being drawn to that table with a sick fascination as if being pulled by a magnet. Underneath were magazines about astrology, the occult and Satan. They had pentagrams and pictures of demons and other satanic material that I was repulsed by, yet drawn to; I later realized that they were demonic in nature.

Fear colored so many of my earliest memories and recollections because I now understand that these magazines and books acted as open portals/doors for evil spirits, namely, the spirit of fear, to enter our home and then into me through their very presence in our house. I have always loved words, books, and printed materials and when I learned how to read, I would read any and everything I could get my hands on. I also recall sitting in our living room even watching snippets of horror movies such as The Omen, Amityville Horror and other movies glorifying demonic activities. Although I wasn't allowed to watch these movies, I did anyway because I was sneaky. After being exposed to these demonic forces, my entire outlook on life changed. As a matter of fact, I lived my life as a response to fear. The Spirit of Fear took hold in my life and took root so deeply that fear became my constant companion and crippled me in the most basic ways. As I think back, almost everything that happened to me had some element of fear attached. I was afraid of the dark, afraid of confrontation, afraid of pain, afraid to be alone, afraid of relationships, afraid to be open and honest, afraid to be "normal", just simply afraid. Fear was so much a part of me that I had and have issues recognizing who I really am in the Lord. Doubt and Fear has been successful up until now even in my thoughts about what I can be, have and do!

2 Timothy 1:7 says *God has not given us the "spirit of fear"* but as a child, I was very fearful, almost to the point of torment. Looking back, some of my earliest memories are clouded by fear and anxiety. Since God did not give me this spirit then it could only come from the one who hates me and desires to see me sifted as wheat, Satan. I can remember my parents fighting late at night during a thunderstorm (which was another great fear for me). I have an image in my mind of the light fixture in our dining room swaying back and forth as the thunder boomed outside while angry screams and curses flew back and forth accompanied by running footsteps, shaking the ceiling inside of my home. I believe that this event heralded where my fear of confrontation came from later on in my life. I became a pacifist because I was so afraid of confrontation. I was in one fight as a child (which I lost) and was terrified of being hurt by punches, scratches and blows. I learned to avoid *any* type of confrontation at all costs and made pacifism (my flawed idea of perfection) my goal in all areas of my life. I cultivated being a pacifist and not making waves even when by rights I should have stood up for myself. This is when I became a people pleaser. I was

often depressed and unhappy because I expected people to know what I wanted and to do the right thing by me.

Fear causes us to settle for far less than God's will for our lives. Jer. 29:11 NIV *For I know the plans I have for you," declares the LORD, "plans to prosper you and not to harm you, plans to give you hope and a future.* Existing in a state of fear guarantees a life devoid of peace and joy. During my personal journey, I've sought peace and joy and could never attain them on my own no matter what I attempted to do. I did not find them in relationships, money, sex, alcohol, or escapism, nothing that I did gave me what my spirit craved.

Make it PERSONAL

As you navigate this journey of discovery, it's important to understand that the spirit of fear is a bully and wants to make you shrink back from every good and perfect gift that Abba has for your life and your lineage. As in my life, fear is usually introduced at an early age and has its own unique source. If you are having trouble uncovering the source of the fear - turn to Holy Spirit- He will lead you and guide you into all truth. If necessary, seek counseling and never neglect being in the presence of our Father. Remember, you must get to the root to destroy the fruit.

Questions to Ponder:

1. Are you governed by fear? Do you allow circumstances of what you think *may* happen to keep you from moving forward?

2. Make a list of any/all occurrences from your childhood that could be possible portals for demonic influence to enter your life.

Insecurity

Insecurity is defined as (1) uncertainty or anxiety about oneself; lack of confidence. (2) the state of being open to danger or threat; lack of protection. Closely allied with insecurity is rejection. Rejection is defined as "not given approval or acceptance." We will explore how these two partner together to dominate the lives of believers. 1 Peter 2:4 NLT *You are coming to Christ, who is the living cornerstone of God's temple. He was rejected by people, but he was chosen by God for great honor.*

These two, insecurity and rejection, together can often spell doom in the lives of people. Insecurity can manifest in many different ways, but we see it at its worst when the person affected is anxious, always looking for approval from others, cannot make decisions, and comes off as "needy" in relationships. This person may also be consumed with jealousy and envy towards others and in relationships, attempts to keep the significant other close at all times even to the point of severing family ties and other close friendships. These signs are red flags and are the traits often found in abusers in domestic violence situations. Those who are insecure are often tormented by thoughts of inferiority and are constantly seeking attention and approval from anyone who will provide it. The Father says in His Word, **"What** *is man, that thou art mindful of him?"* Well, not only was He thinking about us, but He showered us with an incomprehensible love when He sent His Only Son to die for us! This assurance provides us with all we need to overcome insecurity in our lives. Psalm 139:14 (KJV) *I will praise thee; for I am fearfully and wonderfully made: marvelous are thy works; and that my soul knoweth right well.* Our Father is speaking and speaks into our lives daily and ministers to us through the precious Holy Spirit who whispers softly that we are His beloved! Glory to God! Blessed be the name of our Most High King! He regards us with love and tenderness even in our lowest state! His love is extended towards all mankind, the sinner as-well-as the saint. That is amazing news! When we look upon ourselves to disparage what His hands have made, we need to repent because He calls us wonderful! When we act in this fashion, we call God a liar, God forbid and have mercy! We have a high priest who knows our infirmities. We find in Genesis 1:27(NKJV), the ultimate confirmation, *So God created* *man in His* **own** *image; in the image of God He created him; male and female He created them.* These negative attitudes about ourselves come directly from our enemy who wishes to put on a full assault against our minds! We are warned in John 10:10 (KJV) *that the thief cometh not, but for to steal, and to kill, and to destroy: I am come that they might have life, and that they might have it more abundantly.* We must remember that our adversary wishes nothing but death and destruction over our lives, so stay strong in the Lord and live off of every word that proceeds from the mouth of God! This revelation leads to John 8:32 (KJV) *And ye shall know the truth, and the truth shall make you free.* The truth of the Word of God is so liberating! He allows us to be made free through the knowledge of His Holy Word which He will enlighten to us when we diligently seek to fully know Him!

Finally, every insecurity we have as Christians is dismantled when we consider the beautiful words of our Master in Jeremiah 29:11(KJV) *For I know the thoughts that I think toward you, saith the Lord, thoughts of peace, and not of evil, to give you an expected end.*

MY STRUGGLE WITH INSECURITY

The next root deals with how insecurity came into my life and proceeded to cripple my self-esteem and abort my destiny and purpose. Closely allied with insecurity is rejection. I always had a nagging suspicion that no matter what I did, said, or thought, that I could never measure up to certain standards in my own eyes and in the perceptions of others. One of my greatest needs as a child was to feel secure and confident that those people I loved the most would provide a place of security for me.

Initially, I felt these intruders most keenly in my own family. My older brother and sister would tease me mercilessly about my large, wide lips. This was not done to hurt me, it was never their intention, but as a child I was crushed. The enemy understands that and he uses it in a masterful way to cause doubt and sorrow to creep in. I became so unhappy with my appearance that I attempted to (in my mind) mask what I perceived as a flaw by disfiguring my own body.

When a person has or experiences uncertainty or anxiety about him/herself it leads directly to being open to threat or danger. This threat or danger can come from without or within. In my case, insecurity began as a seed in my own mind. I never felt that I was enough, not pretty enough, not shapely enough, my hair was nappy, my lips were too wide, my nose too big, my legs too skinny. I was a walking example of self-hate and insecurity. I hated my smile, and found fault with just about everything that made me unique and distinctive. I could find no proof that I measured up to my own standard of beauty or anyone else's. I hated to smile, thought that I was ugly and was so broken emotionally that I began to peel the skin from my bottom lip in a desperate attempt to make it appear smaller, but; instead brought more attention to it, because I lost pigmentation and the contrast between my upper and lower lip was even more pronounced. This preoccupation with this one part of my body developed into a general dissatisfaction with my overall appearance and a secret yearning to be like someone else.

Never satisfied with what I saw in my mirror, I compared myself to other girls continuously. As a consequence of my insecurity, I had much difficulty in developing sound friendships. I did not have childhood friends because of my mother's distrust of other people, so my siblings were those who I bonded with and built my view of friendship on. I remember having a good friend in high school and was so broken that I was challenged because she had other friends. My jealousy and insecurity caused me to spread rumors about personal matters that I was privy to and caused irreparable damage. As I think back now, I understand the hurt and pain that I caused and am Godly sorry for it. Also, as a teenager and young adult this belief caused me to engage in sexual behaviors that were risky and demeaning. I felt that in order to be accepted that I had to participate in sexual activity whether I desired it or not. My self-worth was so low that I offered my body in exchange for acceptance and what I thought was love. I had an unhealthy desire to please others at my own expense.

"Know ye not, that your body is the temple of the Lord?" My insecurity led me to a place of deep depression and a desire to be free of my reality. Thank God I never wanted to kill myself because the fear of death had an equally strong grip on my mind. I was caught in between

two crippling emotions and didn't know how to break free. I was too afraid to tell my parents how I felt and was also too afraid to tell my siblings how they were making me feel. I now see that there were so many generational strongholds and iniquities at work in my family that only the love of God would have been able to deliver us from the bondage.

Make it PERSONAL

Insecurity keeps you in a place of half-in, half out with God, others and even yourself. You are unable to trust that God has made you perfectly you. In our quest to please people due to our insecurities- we can negate the plan that God has for our lives. In order to uncover the root of Insecurity, it may be necessary to go on an intentional fast and seek the Lord on how to uncover the root in order to be made free.

1. What are some behaviors that you see in yourself that point to insecurity?

2. How do you view yourself? Do you compare yourself to others in unhealthy ways?

3. Are you challenged by others who demonstrate a strong sense of self - confidence?

Rejection

Rejection is a sneaky and crippling demon that partners with Insecurity. Rejection can also lead to depression, self-harm and thoughts of suicide. I can also speak to how rejection made my junior high years pure torture. Coming up, we were poor, I didn't realize just how poor until I was around people who made me aware that what I possessed did not "measure up". My clothing and shoes were not name-brand. We couldn't afford those things that others had. My hair was not permed. I was skinny and awkward. You can imagine how my 7th and 8th grade years went. I desperately wanted to fit in with the cool kids but that was not happening, so I tried to fit in with the smart kids.

It just so happened that the cool kids were also the smart kids. Surprisingly, the only thing that kept me from going crazy was going to church where I was accepted not so much by my peers but by the adults because of my zeal. Jesus knows all of the sufferings and sin that is common to man.

The Bible says in Matthew 21:42 AMPC, *Jesus asked them, have you never read in the Scriptures: The very Stone which the builders rejected and threw away has become the Cornerstone; this is the Lord's doing, and it is marvelous in our eyes?* I caution myself to never forget that even though I sometimes still feel the sting of rejection, that Jesus was scorned and rejected by the ones who should have known Him as the conquering King. Since I identify with Christ, I too will feel rejection, but God is faithful and will place Godly people in my life so that we may sharpen each other. And just in case everyone forsakes me for His cause; He never will!

My personal battle with Rejection, unfortunately, did not end during my adolescence, but continued into my adulthood, even until the past few months. I'd find myself seeking approval from people that I knew didn't like me and meant me no good. As a young teen, I never had a place that I fit. During P.E. classes, (I hated P.E.) I was chosen last for team participation and because I was not athletic, I invariably lost or gave away points for the team. So, I can remember the beginnings of people pleasing taking root in me.

Pleasing people is extremely dangerous because it takes you outside of the will of God. My Apostle, Tony Wade, coined the phrase, "Living to please the audience of One": that One being our Lord and Savior,

Jesus Christ! I should seek His approval above all others! I find my identity in His love and approval of and for me as I walk in His perfect will for my life. He is the only one who deserves my adoration, respect, unwavering obedience, and love. He is the one who holds my life and destiny and knows my appointed end. I am so grateful to God for the newness of life and the sisters who are true friends that He has placed in my life. They encourage me, exhort me, love me, challenge me, rebuke me, and are obedient to the call of the Lord upon their lives.

Make it PERSONAL

As you continue on this journey to freedom from Rejection and its partners, there are some questions that you must reflect on and be ready to war with.

1. Why do I do what I do?

2. Am I looking for approval from others above and beyond approval from God?

3. Do I look to others for constant validation? What is my response if I don't receive this validation that I seek?

4. Do I spend time considering whether my actions will cause a certain response in others?

5. Have you found yourself struggling with depression, self-harm or suicidal thoughts?

When researching this definition, it was interesting to note that Offense is defined as "the condition of," to be/*feel* offended, take exception, take something personally, *feel* affronted, be/*feel* resentful, take something amiss, take umbrage, be/get/*feel* upset, be/get/*feel* annoyed, be/get/*feel* angry, get into a huff." The operative word in each of the definitions is "*feel.*" Now this is the kicker, Pride often rides shotgun with Offense. Pride will keep the offended person from being humble enough to pull the brother/sister aside for a frank discussion.

Look at how much damage and destruction that can come from the misuse of our feelings or emotions. When we allow ourselves to live at the mercy of our emotions, we are in danger of never reaching our full potential. The Bible cautions us to be angry, but sin not. This lets us know that emotions have their proper place in our lives but if we live from our souls they can define and defile us if we are not careful.

Proverbs 18:19 KJV *A brother offended is harder to be won than a strong city: and their contentions are like the bars of a castle.* This scripture bears a little background to be completely understood. Historically, a "strong city" was one that was built on a hill and surrounded by some type of wall in order to fortify it against attacks. The placement on the hill was an advantage since anyone seeking to do harm would be spotted from a distance, allowing time for a proper defense to be mounted. Generally, these fortifications could only be overcome by an aggressor who was ready to hunker down and "starve them out." So, the take- away is that an offended person has built walls and scenarios around the event that can hardly be breached. Their vantage point of Offense leaves them in a place where love, reason, and forgiveness can not enter in. The following scriptural references give us an insight into the heart and mind of God and his instructions on how to properly handle the offenses which will come in our lives. There is no way to live this life and not have offense come, however; offense is not only manageable but able to be overcome when handled with the Word of God. There are three important points to consider when dealing with Offense, either your own or your brothers:

*We must understand that our emotions will lie to us.

*We must understand that our adversary, the devil, wants us in a place of unforgiveness and bitterness so that he can accuse us before the Father, our righteous judge.

* We must understand that God places His Word above His Name, so it is imperative that we know what He says concerning Offense.

Prov. 19:11 (ESV) *Good sense makes one slow to anger, and it is his glory to overlook an offense.* We must learn how to just let some things go! We do not have to give an ear to everything that happens to us or is brought to us. Some events are best just to be forgiven and forgotten.

This next verse continues in the same vein, sometimes we "look" for reasons to be offended, but the Word of God says in Ecc. 7:21-22 KJV *Also take no heed unto all words that are spoken; lest thou hear thy servant curse thee: For oftentimes also thine own heart knoweth that thou thyself likewise hast cursed others.* This verse is also a caution against being hypocritical in nature, and reminds us that we too have been caught up in error. Matt. 18:15-17 NLT *"If another believer sins against you, go privately and point out the offense. If the other person listens and confesses it, you have won that person back.*

This is where so much confusion begins in the House of the Lord, when we rebelliously decide that we are going to talk about the situation with someone else other than the person who is directly involved. A simple matter that could be straightened out with a frank discussion between the two parties turns into discord and chaos! A situation occurred just this year in my life where someone was offended by an innocent comment that I made over two years ago! I had no idea that I had hurt that person with my words and it caused strife and division that could have been easily remedied with a conversation that day. The Father is clear on how He views this in Proverbs 6:16-19 KJV. *These six things doth the Lord hate: yea, seven are an abomination unto him: 17 A proud look, a lying tongue, and hands that shed innocent blood, 18 An heart that deviseth wicked imaginations, feet that be swift in running to mischief, 19 A false witness that speaketh lies, and he that* **soweth discord** *among brethren.* The Lord hates the one who sows discord! Beware, my brothers and sisters!

James 3:16 KJV *for where envying and strife is, there is confusion and every evil work.* This strife that the Bible speaks of oftentimes stems from our disobedience and disregard for, or lack of knowledge about the Word. We must strive to hide the Word of God in our hearts so that we don't sin against Him! This means that we must spend quality time in study of the Word in order to apply it to our lives. This is the only way that our lives will be transformed and changed to His glory! He says be ye transformed by the renewing of your minds! The Word of God is the only vehicle through the power of Holy Ghost that has the ability to change us from the inside out! Hallelujah! To God be the Glory!

Sometimes, valid offenses come and we wonder, how long do we have to deal with a person who seems to be using us or misusing us; the answer lies in Luke 17:3-4 KJV *3 Take heed to yourselves: If thy brother trespass against thee, rebuke him; and if he repent, forgive him. 4 And if he trespass against thee seven times in a day, and seven times in a day turn again to thee, saying, I repent; thou shalt forgive him.* The ultimate answer lies in who we are in Christ. Have we cultivated the Fruit of the Spirit? Do we truly possess self-control, long-suffering and patience? Have we grown these fruits by dwelling in the presence of the Lord and putting our flesh on the cross?

Finally, James gives us some advice that if heeded, will result in the desired outcome; the mastery over offense.

James 1:19 KJV *Wherefore, my beloved brethren, let every man be swift to hear, slow to speak, slow to wrath.* Love nullifies offense. We can rest in the assurance that the love of God will allow us to achieve victory over offense and every other situation that could separate us from the Father. 1 Cor. 13:1-13 ERV *I may speak in different languages, whether human or even of angels. But if I don't have love, I am only a noisy bell or a ringing cymbal. 2 I may have the gift of prophecy, I may understand all secrets and know everything there is to know, and I may have faith so great that I can move mountains. But even with all this, if I don't have love, I am nothing. 3 I may give away everything I have to help others, and I may even give my body as an offering to be burned. But I gain nothing by doing all this if I don't have love. 4 Love is patient and kind. Love is not jealous, it does not brag, and it is not proud. 5 Love is not rude, it is not selfish, and it cannot be made angry easily. Love does not remember wrongs done against it. 6 Love is never happy when others do wrong, but it is always happy with the truth. 7 Love never gives up on people. It never stops trusting, never loses hope, and never quits. 8 Love will never end. But all those gifts will come to an end—even the gift of prophecy, the gift of speaking in different kinds of languages, and the gift of knowledge. 9 These will all end because this knowledge and these prophecies we have are not complete. 10 But when perfection comes, the things that are not complete will end. 11 When I was a child, I talked like a child, I thought like a child, and I made plans like a child. When I became a man, I stopped those childish ways. 12 It is the same with us. Now we see God as if we are looking at a reflection in a mirror. But then, in the future, we will see him right before our eyes. Now I know only a part, but at that time I will know fully, as God has known me. 13 So these three things continue: faith, hope, and love. And the greatest of these is love.* Our daily prayer should be, Father, fill me with your love, so that it overflows from me and spreads through me to reach the world.

An offended person rehearses and relives the real or imagined wrong, creating scenarios and conversations until finally the "incident" which caused the offense has grown into a mountain-sized obstacle. The Bible speaks on how to properly handle offense, but as a child, I knew nothing of the Word of God and how to apply it to my life. My family was unchurched up until I was 12 years of age. Our norm was to attend church on Easter Sundays, and I recall these excursions occurring only after we moved to Memphis in 1977.

Although we were somewhat morally sound, we had no Biblical truth to guide our lives. Satan does not fight fair and sought to destroy my life as a small child. I spent my childhood at the mercy of my flawed emotions, the flawed emotions of those around me and my equally flawed responses to them. I vividly remember an incident where I was beaten harshly for no reason (or so I assumed). I was so hurt and upset that I allowed the event to run in endless cycles in my mind. My little sister wanted some jello, so my daddy told me to give her some. I was in a huff because I didn't want to be disturbed (I was in the wrong). So I gave her the jello on a saucer and went back to what I was doing. She made a mess (because I put it in a saucer instead of a bowl). Of course, I received a whipping.

My offense with my daddy turned into the beginnings of a hatred that I hid in my heart towards him. I did not tell my parents how I felt

about anything. And because of the fear that was attached to me I dared not even try. After each rehearsal, my emotions grew stronger and more destructive until they turned into hatred, distrust, and the desire to pretend that my life was different. This example, lumped together with the many other dysfunctional events which were part of my upbringing, led me to develop these destructive and chaotic emotions. I often found myself turning to reading as an outlet and built an imaginary life that I could escape to when my own reality became too much to bear. This reliance on escapism led me to engage in reading material that was wicked in nature and which in turn began the stirrings of lust, perversion and eventually to an addiction to pornographic material.

One sin leads to another and eventually the path quickens toward destruction. Oh yeah, the doctrine of "once saved always saved." A complete and utter lie. For the wages of sin is death…. Although I was saved, **my sins** broke fellowship with God and set my feet on the broad path which leads to destruction.

Make it
PERSONAL

If there is anything more destructive than Offense, other than practicing sin, I don't know what it is. Offense is a malignancy like cancerous cells that must be cut out, burned out, eradicated and obliterated by any means necessary. If you find yourself frequently offended, there is deep heart work that must be done. When a person is offended, they live as if time is on their side - it is not.

1. Why am I bothered by what someone says or does either to me or about me?

2. What is the position of my heart towards God and towards His people? Do I have a victim's mentality and how does that impact my thought life?

3. What are my "triggers" and how do they affect my life?

4. Do I seek to get people "on my side" when speaking of situations/circumstances?

Bitterness

This vile root is so insidious that I didn't even realize it was there in my heart – poisoning relationships, and keeping me chained to old hurts and disappointments. Bitterness is defined as; hurt, resentment, anger and hate. It can be caused by a person or an experience. It often begins (in its seed form) as an offense, a "wrong" or a "perceived wrong", or even an intentional wrong. It is fertilized when the victim feels resentment towards the perpetrator and instead of practicing Biblical Forgiveness, continues to rehearse and live in that place of hurt. Bitterness can also be a learned behavior, remember; children and unfortunately many adults model the negative actions and attitudes that they see practiced. The old saying, "what goes in, must come out" is true both in the natural and the spirit realm.

Hebrews 12:15 (AMPC), states, *Exercise foresight and be on the watch to look [after one another], to see that no one falls back from and fails to secure God's grace (His unmerited favor and spiritual blessing),* **in order that no root of resentment (rancor, bitterness, or hatred) shoots forth and causes trouble and bitter torment, and the many become contaminated and defiled by it—** Ephesians 4:31(AMPC) *Let all bitterness and indignation and wrath (passion, rage, bad temper) and resentment (anger, animosity) and quarreling (brawling, clamor, contention) and slander (evil-speaking, abusive or blasphemous language) be banished from you, with all malice (spite, ill will, or baseness of any kind).*

The two previous scriptures point to the implications for bitterness and how it can manifest in our lives; while Romans 12: 17-21 provide us with the remedy for dealing with wounded and broken hearts. Romans 12: 17-21 (AMPC) *Repay no one evil for evil, but take thought for what is honest and proper and noble [aiming to be above reproach] in the sight of everyone. 18 If possible, as far as it depends on you, live at peace with everyone. 19 Beloved, never avenge yourselves, but leave the way open for [God's] wrath; for it is written, Vengeance is Mine, I will repay (requite), says the Lord. 20 But if your enemy is hungry, feed him; if he is thirsty, give him drink; for by so doing you will heap burning coals upon his head. 21 Do not let yourself be overcome by evil, but overcome (master) evil with good.*

I was bitter about many situations in my life but was in denial about it. I regarded it as me being the victim of so many circumstances -a product of my parents' dysfunctional relationship, financial instability, my failed marriage, single parenthood, lack of confidence, etc., etc., etc. It was not until I took ownership of my own life and the choices that I made, that I became aware that I could trace my issues back to unforgiven offenses that came from my past. These grew into bitterness that spread like a vine in almost every area of my life. This Bitterness acted as a poison that resulted in me being envious of the lives of those around me. I could not understand why my path seemed so hard and others were living "the life." I struggled with making poor choices (financially, relationally, emotionally and physically), time after time that led me deeper into poverty and debt, naturally and spiritually.

Because I was so fearful and struggled with insecurity, I never felt as if anything would work for me. I remember in my early 20's, I was pressured into becoming a Mary Kay Rep. I really enjoyed the presentation and the potential for prosperity that being successful in the business stood for. I purchased the materials but then doubt and fear crept in and convinced me that I was too undeserving to step out and let the product sell itself. As I am writing this, Holy Spirit is bringing this back to my remembrance. This was another experience that I had buried in my secret spot, my heart. I was just too afraid of rejection and of failure and therefore could not push past the barrier to success.

Make it PERSONAL

Here are some helpful questions to assist you in uncovering bitterness in your own heart.

1. Does the thought of someone's prosperity make you envious, jealous or to behave in a belittling fashion?
2. How do you react when someone you deem lesser than you is excelling in life?
3. Do you actively speak against them or call their successes "little" or do you secretly hope for their demise or downfall?

If the answers to any of these questions are yes, then immediately repent and seek deliverance! Remember, bitterness is like cancerous growths, in order to eradicate the disease, you must change the environment that it inhabits.

Pride

Each time I hear the word pride, I'm instantly reminded of the old adage - pride goes before a fall. Normally, people only consider the outside trappings of pride and how a person who is caught in its trap will somehow be brought low. Usually that attitude is directed outward in a "gotcha" type situation instead of inward in an attitude of self-reflection and repentance. Pride is a very tricky and subtle spirit because of its connotation. There are so many worldly and wicked forms of pride, National pride, parental pride, black pride, white pride, gay pride, the list goes on and on. When pride is couched in these terms, it seems as if it is a good thing, a thing to be desired, admired and fought for. All of the aforementioned types of pride come straight from the enemy's camp. If the Father is against something, you can count on the enemy doing his best to capitalize and ensnare people in it.

Pride can be described in terms that make it seem a desirable trait to have but the Believer must be careful because all pride can lead to our greatest downfall. What is pride? Pride is defined as a feeling of deep pleasure or satisfaction derived from **one's own** achievements, the achievements of those with whom **one** is closely associated, or from qualities or possessions that are widely admired, synonyms: be proud of, be proud of **oneself** for, take pride in, take satisfaction in, congratulate **oneself** on, pat **oneself** on the back for.

As we examine these definitions, there is a trend that identifies how pride can be unhealthy and very often wicked from the Lord's standpoint. We should not boast about our own accomplishments, because this leads to a sense of entitlement and superiority which causes a God-complex within ourselves. This superiority, which can cause us to become highly judgmental, demeaning and arrogant, stems from a skewed self - perception that allows our thoughts, ideas, and actions to overtake and outstrip anything that anyone else can accomplish. Each "win" or achievement leads to an ever more heightened opinion of ourselves. Soon, the person believes that they have all sufficiency in every matter and that there is no need for God because of the false belief that "I" can do it all on/in my own power. You have now taken God's Glory! This view causes us to make God into a liar because the Word says that I can do all things through Christ who strengthens me. God refers to such a person as stiff-necked, puffed up, and ultimately damned.

In fact, pride is mentioned at least 46 times in the KJV. There is a wealth of scriptural reference on this topic because of its importance in our lives. I'm almost overwhelmed by including so many scriptures but Holy Spirit is leading me to include these. This will help us to meditate on His Word and the principles that are contained herein that will keep us from falling to the leviathan of pride. I have attempted to place each scripture under a corresponding heading. As you read through these, take a critical look at your own life and your attitude. Do you see yourself in any of these verses? I have included the problem, God's viewpoint and the way of escape.

Pride in Self

1 John 2:16 NIV *For everything in the world--the lust of the flesh, the lust of the eyes, and the pride of life--comes not from the Father but from the world*

1 Cor. 8:2 NIV *Those who think they know something do not yet know as they ought to know.*

Psalm 10:4 NIV *In his pride the wicked man does not seek him; in all his thoughts there is no room for God*

Prov. 26:12 NIV *Do you see a person wise in their own eyes? There is more hope for a fool than for them.*

Prov. 16:18 NIV *Pride goes before destruction, a haughty spirit before a fall.*

Phil. 2:3 NIV *Do nothing out of selfish ambition or vain conceit. Rather, in humility value others above yourselves,*

2 Cor. 10:18 NIV *For it is not the one who commends himself who is approved, but the one whom the Lord commends*

2 Tim.3:2 NIV *People will be lovers of themselves, lovers of money, boastful, proud, abusive, disobedient to their parents, ungrateful, unholy*

WHAT GOD SAYS AGAINST PRIDE

1 Peter 5:5 NIV *In the same way, you who are younger, submit yourselves to your elders. All of you, clothe yourselves with humility toward one another, because, "God opposes the proud but shows favor to the humble."*

Prov.6:16-17 NIV *There are six things the LORD hates, seven that are detestable to him: haughty eyes, (a proud look) a lying tongue, hands that shed innocent blood*

Mark 7:20-23 NIV *He went on: "What comes out of a person is what defiles them. For it is from within, out of a person's heart, that evil thoughts come -sexual immorality, theft, murder, adultery, greed, malice, deceit, lewdness, envy, slander, arrogance and folly. All these evils come from inside and defile a person."*

Prov. 8:13 NIV *To fear the LORD is to hate evil; I hate pride and arrogance, evil behavior and perverse speech*

Prov. 16:5 NIV *The LORD detests all the proud of heart. Be sure of this: They will not go unpunished.*

Gal. 6:3-4 NIV *If anyone thinks they are something when they are not, they deceive themselves. Each one should test their own actions. Then they can take pride in themselves alone, without comparing themselves to someone else,*

Psalm 59:12 NIV *For the sins of their mouths, for the words of their lips, let them be caught in their pride. For the curses and lies they utter,*

Luke 18:9-14 ERV *There were some people who thought they were very good and looked down on everyone else. Jesus used this story to teach them: 10 "One time there was a Pharisee and a tax collector. One day they both went to the Temple to pray. 11 The Pharisee stood alone, away from the tax collector. When the Pharisee prayed, he said, 'O God, I thank you that I am not as bad as other people. I am not like men who steal, cheat, or commit adultery. I thank you that I am better than this tax collector. 12 I fast twice a week, and I give a tenth of everything I get!' 13 "The tax collector stood alone too. But when he prayed, he would not even look up to heaven. He felt very humble before God. He said, 'O God, have mercy on me. I am a sinner!' 14 I tell you, when this man finished his prayer and went home, he was right with God. But the Pharisee, who felt that he was better than others, was not right with God. People who make themselves important will be made humble. But those who make themselves humble will be made important."* Pride gives us a false sense of importance!

PRIDE AGAINST THE LORD

2 Kings 19:22 NIV *Who is it you have ridiculed and blasphemed? Against whom have you raised your voice and lifted your eyes in pride? Against the Holy One of Israel!*

OVERCOMING PRIDE

Prov. 29:23 NIV *Pride brings a person low, but the lowly in spirit gain honor.*

Prov. 13:10 NIV *Where there is strife, there is pride, but wisdom is found in those who take advice*

Isaiah 66:1-2 NIV *This is what the LORD says: "Heaven is my throne, and the earth is my footstool. Where is the house you will build for me? Where will my resting place be? Has not my hand made all these things, and so they came into being?" declares the LORD. "These are the ones I look on with favor: those who are humble and contrite in spirit, and who tremble at my word.*

Rom. 12:16 NIV *Live in harmony with one another. Do not be proud, but be willing to associate with people of low position. Do not be conceited.*

Prov.11:2 NIV *When pride comes, then comes disgrace, but with humility comes wisdom.*

James 4:6 NIV *But he gives us more grace. That is why Scripture says: "God opposes the proud but shows favor to the humble."*

Prov. 18:12 NIV *Before a downfall the heart is haughty, but humility comes before honor*

Prov. 27:2 NIV *Let someone else praise you, and not your own mouth; an outsider, and not your own lips.*

MY DOWNFALL

Growing up, I was taught to be prideful, not in an intentionally bad way, but because in our flesh dwells no good thing, my sin nature took on arrogance, boastfulness and a superiority complex. My mom had good intentions but would compare us (my siblings) in a harmful manner by saying things like, "Karen, is the smartest one of my children." I took pride in the label and the knowledge that I was indeed the smartest one. My selfish and (unfounded) pride led to my downfall.

Academically, I thought that I knew it all and that mindset persisted for many years, until I was confronted with the truth that there were many people who were truly gifted, in Jr. & Sr. High and I did not equal up. When I realized that fact, pride kept my mouth shut from receiving help when I desperately needed it. Instead of telling my parents that I was struggling, I changed my grades on my report cards (lying and cheating), and they never knew the difference. It's disgusting how one sin leads to another, and self deception is the worst type of sin. How can you ever get free if you believe your own lies?

Those old feelings of superiority try to come to the surface and even now, I must be intentional about putting my flesh on the cross and dying daily to pride! As I write this, I am constantly in awe of how much God loved me, loves me and will forever love me. He waited for me to answer His call and pulled me out of my self-imposed prison and set me free!

Make it PERSONAL

Pride is so sneaky and subtle and can appear in your life in small ways that can have disastrous outcomes.

1. Ask Holy Spirit to reveal to you areas/instances in your life that are not pleasing to Him. As He reveals them to you, be quick to repent and put in place measures that will keep pride from gaining a foothold in your life. What area will you begin with?

2. In my life, I use 2 verses that serve as a heart check. Philippians 2:5, Let this mind be in you which was also in Christ Jesus: and Psalm 51:10 Create in me a clean heart, O God: and renew a right spirit within me. Memorize these verses.

Sexual Immorality

Defined: Webster's Dictionary defines perversion as "diverting from the true intent or purpose; a change to something worse; a turning or applying to a wrong end or use." Let it be stated that sex is intended solely for the married couple - (one man joined to one woman). One Christian marital counselor states, "Anything which degrades the other partner such as enacting or promoting rape fantasies, in my view, cannot take place as part of a healthy, sexual, marital relationship." Neither partner should treat the other as a slave or a child, an animal or an object.

The Bible also refers to perversion as immorality and or the "works of the flesh." An immoral person is one who acts contrary to or does not obey or conform to standards, evil or licentious behavior- " the lusts of the flesh, the pride of life."

The Bible speaks of our bodies as temples of the Lord and that our reasonable service is to remain chaste until marriage. Even after marriage we should be careful to keep only to our spouses in deed and in thought.

Before we proceed any further on this topic, I'd like to be very clear. All sin is abhorrent to God, he hates the sin but loves the sinner. Having said that, it is my intent to also treat this subject matter from the lens of God's love for the sinner, and His inability to allow sin to be in His holy presence.

As a youngster, I fell prey to sexually suggestive material and pornography which invaded and perverted my mind, my soul and my body. I've mentioned previously that I would read anything that I got my hands on. So, one day at school in the 5th grade, there was a "dirty book" that was being passed around and whispered about, and finally, it was my turn to take it home and read it. At that point, I hadn't seen any nude photos and had very little knowledge of the male and female anatomy, so I had blurred images in my mind of what I was reading. I was overwhelmed by the thoughts and urges that were awakened in me and that I was incapable of handling as an adult, let alone as a young child. So the seed of perversion was planted in my soul (mind, will, and emotions) and I was consumed by it. When my obsession led me to move from printed text to looking at pornographic magazines (which my older brother had a roomful of) I then had solid images to base my

wonderings on. The filthy words and images in that book came to vivid color, one hot summer day when I trespassed (another sin) in my brother's room and found his hidden stash of magazines.

In the life of a Christian, the most detrimental sins are those sins committed against your own body. 1 Corinthians 6:19 AMPC *Do you not know that your body is the temple (the very sanctuary) of the Holy Spirit Who lives within you, whom you have received [as a Gift] from God? You are not your own,*

When Jesus died, the veil in the Temple was split in half from top to bottom, signifying the removal of the curse of the law and the ushering in of Grace. One of the hardest restrictions about the law was that we did not have access to the Father because of our sinful state. In fact, even the High Priest could only enter behind the veil once a year at the time of Atonement. The finished work of the cross meant that we no longer needed a blood offering (bulls, goats, sheep) to atone for our sins! Glory to God!

The blood of Jesus was and is the ultimate and final sacrifice which allows us to come boldly before the Throne of Grace and into the Presence of Almighty God! Willfully engaging in sexual sin, creates a barrier that Holy Spirit will not cross. Whenever we sin intentionally it grieves Holy Spirit and He will not dwell in an unclean temple. After Jesus died, the physical Temple was no longer needed because the Lord could now dwell within us! Bless His Holy Name! That is why we are referred to as the Body of Christ, He (Jesus) being the Head!!

The Bible goes on to say that this is our reasonable service. Reasonable means, having sound judgment; fair and sensible, and as much as is appropriate or fair; moderate. So, it is appropriate for us to abstain from sexual impurity: if unmarried it's called fornication, if you're married it's called adultery.

Another term which goes hand in hand with sexual impurity is immorality. Immoral means one who acts contrary to or does not obey or conform to standards (prescribed standards in the Word of God), evil or licentious behavior. In the natural world, we are only aware of the physical consequences of partaking in unsanctioned sex; depression, unwanted pregnancy(ies), disease, broken and chaotic relationships, and financial ruin. All of these issues are bad enough within themselves but when the law of God attaches, it becomes damning. There are other even more devastating consequences to immoral behavior such as soul ties and abortion. These can cause long-term relational consequences that can adversely affect every potential relationship in the future.

The true Marriage Covenant that God instituted, can only be entered into by one man and one woman. ALL other configurations fall into the category of perversion. Same sex attraction, to include homosexuality and lesbianism is an abomination to God because it perverts the proper use of the body that God created in His own image and after His own likeness. God created women to be receivers and men to be givers, it is evident in the design of the body. Women receive the sperm and in the process conception occurs so that new life will come forth. God also created sex as a binder to strengthen the marital ties and to cause those two individuals to become one and because He loves us so much; He made it a pleasurable act.

God is a God of decency, order, holiness and righteousness, and operates eternally so. We are living in an age where any and everything goes, there is no black and white - too many blurred lines. But God does not change, His Word will not fail, it is just and true, because He is just and true.

Perversion is fueled by lust and wicked imaginings born in an unredeemed soul, spirit and flesh. Don't get it twisted, sin is abhorrent to God and He can not and will not abide by it. So following in the same vein, bestiality, orgies, masturbation, threesomes, pornography etc. are all against the will and plan of God for our temples.

Acts 15:29 NKJV *that you abstain from things offered to idols, from blood, from things strangled, and from sexual immorality. If you keep yourselves from these, you will do well. Farewell.*

1 Cor. 5: 1-5, NKJV *It is actually reported that there is sexual immorality among you, and such sexual immorality as is not even named among the Gentiles-that a man has his father's wife! 2 And you are puffed up, and have not rather mourned, that he who has done this deed might be taken away from among you. 3 For I indeed, as absent in body but present in spirit, have already judged (as though I were present) him who has so done this deed. 4 In the name of our Lord Jesus Christ, when you are gathered together, along with my spirit, with the power of our Lord Jesus Christ, 5 deliver such a one to Satan for the destruction of the flesh, that his spirit may be saved in the day of the Lord Jesus.*

1 Corinthians 5:9-11 NKJV *I wrote to you in my epistle not to keep company with sexually immoral people. 10 Yet I certainly did not mean with the sexually* *immoral people of this world, or with the covetous, or extortioners, or idolaters, since then you would need to go out of the world. 11 But now I have written to you not to keep company with anyone named a brother, who is sexually immoral, or covetous, or an idolater, or a reviler, or a drunkard, or an extortioner-not even to eat with such a person.*

1 Corinthians 6:9-11 NKJV *Do you not know that the unrighteous will not inherit the kingdom of God? Do not be deceived. Neither fornicators, nor idolaters, nor adulterers, nor homosexuals, nor sodomites, 10 nor thieves, nor covetous, nor drunkards, nor revilers, nor extortioners will inherit the kingdom of God. 11 And such were some of you. But you were washed, but you were sanctified, but you were justified in the name of the Lord Jesus and by the Spirit of our God.*

1 Corinthians 10:8 NKJV *Nor let us commit sexual immorality, as some of them did, and in one day twenty-three thousand fell;*

Galatians 5:19 NKJV *Now the works of the flesh are evident, which are: adultery, fornication, uncleanness, lewdness*

Ephesians 4:19 NKJV *who, being past feeling, have given themselves over to lewdness, to work all uncleanness with greediness.*

Ephesians 5:3 NKJV *But fornication and all uncleanness of covetousness, let it not even be named among you, as is fitting for saints;*

Jude 1:7 NKJV *as Sodom and Gomorrah, and the cities around them in a similar manner to these, having given themselves over to sexual immorality and gone after strange flesh, are set forth as an example, suffering the vengeance of eternal fire.*

Leviticus 20:13 NKJV *If a man lies with a male as he lies with a woman, both of them have committed an abomination. They shall surely be put to death. Their blood shall be upon them.*

Romans 1:26-27 NKJV *For this reason, God gave them up to vile passions. For even their women exchanged the natural use for what is against nature. 27 Likewise also the men, leaving the natural use of the woman, burned in their lust for one another, men with men committing what is shameful, and receiving in themselves the penalty of their error which was due.*

1 Timothy 1:10 NKJV *for fornicators, for sodomites, for kidnappers, for liars, for perjurers, and if there is any other thing that is contrary to sound doctrine,*

Hebrews 13:4 NKJV *Marriage is honorable among all, and the bed undefiled; but fornicators and adulterers God will judge.*

1 Timothy 1:9-11 NKJV *knowing this: that the law is not made for a righteous person, but for the lawless and insubordinate, for the ungodly and for sinners, for the unholy and profane, for murderers of fathers and murderers of mothers, for manslayers, [10] for fornicators, for sodomites, for kidnappers, for liars, for perjurers, and if there is any other thing that is contrary to sound doctrine, [11] according to the glorious gospel of the blessed God which was committed to my trust.*

My Introduction to Sex

Sometime between fourth and sixth grade ages 9-11, I came face to face with pornography. It began with a "dirty novel" that was passed around by my classmates. The book was ragged, cover torn off, just another book. After reading one page I was consumed with an intense craving to read more. I recall being filled with a sick excitement! It was at that very moment that the Spirit of Perversion entered my life. From that moment on, Perversion & Lust controlled my waking and my sleeping thoughts and left me with no peace. It was as if someone had told me that I was going to Disneyland! I remember sitting in class, unable to concentrate on my lesson, because I was consumed with the need to read more! I took it home, went immediately to my room and read the entire book in one setting.

Holy Spirit was working on my behalf even then, because the next day when it was time to go to school, I attempted to hide the book in my jacket (so obvious) instead of putting it in my backpack. My mother, of course, asks me what was in my jacket and the rest as they say is history. I was ashamed because my Daddy (my earthly father) knew what I was doing more so than anything else and mainly because I got caught. I had no shame or remorse as relates to how my heavenly Father regarded my sin and shame.

After reading that trash, my innocence was completely gone. What happened next was almost inevitable, once the door was opened to perversion, lust came right on in. My mind was never free again until the day that the Lord delivered me more than 30 years later. I became a slave to sexual images, thoughts, and imaginings. My body became alive

and I was beset by demons of lust, I was literally on fire with sexual need. Fear was ever present, so I was afraid to touch myself or explore, so the craving to read about sex was ever present. Whatever my older siblings and my mother read, I read. It was almost as if I developed a radar about trashy novels or novels with explicit sex scenes, I was drawn to them. At this point, I hadn't seen any nude photos and had very little knowledge of the male and female anatomy, so I had blurred images in my mind about what I was reading. The enemy made sure that was a short- lived condition. Around this same time, my older brother had a paper route and would bring his large bag back to the house. He always kept the door to his room locked and booby-trapped against his pesky little sisters. One day, I just happened to figure out how to get in and I entered. His walls and ceilings were literally covered with nude pictures of people engaged in sexual intercourse. My previously imagined images were replaced in living color. I was hooked, entranced, mesmerized, - addicted. Just like that. At every opportunity I would go to his room and lose myself in those images. It was a full-on assault by the enemy on a child who knew right from wrong but was helpless to make the right choice. I was beset by feelings of excitement, paranoia, lust, and fear and they were all too powerful to overcome on my own.

SOUL TIES

A soul tie is an emotional bond or connection that unites you with someone else. You can become bound to a person through your soul. The soul consists of our will, our minds and our emotions. Some signs that point to the presence of a soul tie include:

- Being tormented by thoughts about a person and obsessively wondering about them.
- Being unable to break free from intimate (sexual/emotional) relationships.
- Creating excuses to call or spy on them. *rehearsing times spent together, stalking behaviors
- Grieving excessively over a severed relationship

A soul tie is formed through a close friendship, through vows, commitments and promises, and finally through physical intimacy. Soul ties are necessary in God's perfect plan for our lives. In marriages, it builds and binds the two into one flesh. In families, the soul ties help us to love and show the proper concern and care for our kinfolk. Let's be clear, soul ties are not always bad, God uses them to build healthy and proper relationships in our lives but the enemy seeks to distort and pervert every good thing from our Father. It is vitally important that we have the indwelling of Holy Spirit who will lead and guide us into all truth when we consult Him about every area of our lives. The Bible says to shun the very appearance of evil, so dating outside of healthy Christian boundaries can lead to the development of soul ties. Parents, be careful of allowing your teenagers to have "girlfriends and boyfriends"; these seemingly innocent relationships can lead to brokenness later in life.

    I cringe when I think about all of the men that I gave myself to from a place of brokenness. Every sexual act, left a piece of me with them and a piece of them with me. It's no wonder that I took on mindsets and ideologies that did not belong to me. When our souls merge it's like what happens when you have unprotected sex with someone; there is a transfer that takes place. Demons also transfer! This is so dangerous because demons rarely ever travel alone. Lust, pride, rage, and murder, to name a few ,were living inside of me!

I had to sit and remember with the help of Holy Spirit every man that I was intimate with and repent, plead the blood and denounce those ties in order to break them. Even after you've done this, you must work to renew your mind and put your flesh on the cross in order to walk in true freedom. Remember, there is a God part; and He is faithful to do what He says, then there is our end of the bargain to work out our soul salvation in fear and trembling.

Abortion

Abortion is the destruction of a fetus before or during birth. It is murder. It is wicked and comes from the enemy, whose prime directive is to kill, steal, and destroy life, purpose, and destiny. According to the CDC's Morbidity & Mortality Weekly Report (MMWR) of 2015 there were 638,169 abortions performed on women between the ages of 15 and 44 years of age. These were medically induced abortions that cost the world the inventions, strategies and God-given answers that were in those souls. Multiply those numbers by the years between 1969 and the present when abortion became legalized and imagine the millions of children that were killed and not allowed to bring their value to the Earth. The woman's right to choose was not only a legislation of death but an agenda pandered by the enemy and latched on to by Christians and Non-Christians alike.

The Word of God is so true and is alive, breathing, moving and active whether we receive it or not. Romans 6:23 states, *for the wages of sin is death;* I killed my babies. Had I not been engaging in premarital sex, this death would not have occurred. Not once, not twice, but three times. The first abortion was when I was 19 years old. I was so afraid to have a child outside of wedlock, that I took the coward's way out. I had an abortion and my boyfriend dumped me too. I was so depressed afterwards. The procedure itself was so horrible that I was sick to my soul. The worst part was that at home, no one knew or noticed anything different about me. The next year I met my husband and my son was conceived (once again out of wedlock) but we married in the fall of that same year. This is the hardest part of my story to write because, having said what I said, how in the world could I kill 2 more times?

The second abortion was a result of an extramarital affair. My husband and I were separated and I met someone else, so seven years later there I was again in the abortion clinic. My reasoning? My kids should all have the same father. Lord, have mercy. So. There I was, married (on paper) with two children and living a dissolute life. Needless to say, that relationship ended, he left as well.

Let's fast forward to 1999. My marriage is in shambles, and I'm living pretty much as a free agent. I met a guy that I'm absolutely head over heels "in love with" but once again, I had another abortion. My heart is heavy as I write this. I do not take lightly what I did. Believe me when I say that I have agonized over my choices. Thanks be to God that He is so merciful and gracious even when we don't deserve it. He said in Romans 8:1 KJV, *There is therefore now no condemnation to them which are in Christ Jesus, who walk not after the flesh, but after the Spirit.* God forgave me, but the hard part is forgiving myself.

Masturbation

Masturbation is defined as the stimulation of the genitals with the hand(s) for sexual pleasure. Masturbation can lead to sexual addiction and is also a practice that is forbidden to all unmarried people. Why? First of all because God lists it as sexual immorality. When masturbating, one must have an object (person) who is the target of the images that are necessary to bring the act to fruition. The marriage bed is holy and undefiled therefore sexual gratification is limited to married couples.

Masturbation is an image fueled practice and here we find that pornography or pornographic materials are often used to fuel the imagination. These images are often of women/men that are completely different from the spouse and show sexual practices that may be taboo or perverted. This practice often leads to opening doors for demonic activity in our lives. There are powerful spirits such as lust, that partner with perversion, pedophilia and other defiling spirits that that seek entry into our lives to kill, steal, and destroy. Once again, the Bible says to flee sexual immorality!

As much as I knew about sex, I didn't begin masturbating until after I was married. Let me be very bold and say that even though I was married and could engage in sex, because of the lust spirit, I was never satisfied. When I discovered how to stimulate myself, I was hooked. I would go into Adult stores in search of devices to satisfy my urges. All the while, feeling unclean, but driven to be there by the lusts of my flesh.

Masturbation became a routine part of my life, just like washing my face, brushing my teeth, going to work, it was my normal. This practice persisted until I joined Divine Life Church and Apostle Tony Wade was preaching and then the truth of God's Word came and convicted me. I didn't know that masturbation was a sin. I'm sure that there are many others like me who are unaware of this as a sin. I'm hopeful that this will help the scales fall from your eyes as it did for mine. Was it easy to stop participating in a habit? No. Can you be freed of it? Yes, through a willingness to repent, a turning from wickedness and seeking God for help to overcome. I must guard my eyes, my ears, and my mind from sexual thoughts, images, lyrics etc. because I am vulnerable in that area! I will not willingly place myself in situations where my flesh can take the lead! I can say today, thank God I'm free, but there's a warning! My flesh is NOT saved, therefore; I must die daily and take up my cross!

Fantasy Life

What is a fantasy? *noun* 1. the faculty or activity of imagining things, especially things that are impossible or improbable. Holy Spirit also gave me the word, fake, along with an acronym. The word fake is defined as; *noun* a thing that is not genuine; a forgery or sham. He says that the act or the characteristic of fakeness does not belong in the life of a believer. It causes a sense of entitlement, envy, lust, and a host of other emotional baggage which is designed to destroy destiny.

When one lives in a fantasy/fake life, there is little to no comprehension of what is really occurring in the real world or reality. The fantasy world can become so strong and dominant until the mind ceases to function with any clarity and that is where mental health is at risk. This can happen to anyone. I placed the topic of Fantasy here, under Sexual Immorality because it's where I struggled with it the most. I now understand that this topic can be one that stands alone on its own merits simply because of the impact that it can have on destiny.

James 1:17 New International Version, 17 Every good and perfect gift is from above, coming down from the Father of the heavenly lights, who does not change like shifting shadows. Once again we see that God gave man good gifts, but here enters Satan, whose job is to steal, kill, and to destroy. Because he has no creative power; he must take the good things which the Father has created and pervert them, thereby causing destruction. The Lord gave us imagination which is the sanctified cousin to fantasy. This is the acronym for fake. It reads thus, a "false attitude which is knowingly entertained."

> **F**: False - fake, insincere, untrue
>
> **A**: Attitude - a settled way of thinking or feeling about someone or something
>
> **K**: Knowingly - deliberately
>
> **E**: Entertained - give attention or consideration to

God created our imaginations in order to envision and receive the destiny that He has already written into our books of life. Most people have perverted the use of this fantastic gift of imagination which God has given us (myself included). I spent countless hours of my life daydreaming about the things which I wanted but was either too afraid or insecure to reach out for. I can recall sitting and thinking and envisioning myself married to men who were no good for me, or even for themselves. I was enamored with the physical appearance of men. I wanted to be held, touched, taken care of, and lulled into a dream which could never have any footing in reality.

As I grew older, I was on the fence about how I was feeling as compared to what I knew to be right. Because I knew that sex outside of marriage was a sin (fornication) I developed this imaginary husband who I used to imagine all sorts of sexual activity with. In my mind, because I called him "husband" that made what I was imagining ok. Wrong.

The Bible says there is a way to man that seems right but in the end leads to destruction. I lived this imaginary life so long that it became a part of me and when I truly gave my life to the Lord, I had to war with it to free myself with the help of Holy Spirit. Even now, I'll find those old ways trying to creep back in and I must put my flesh and my soul on the cross! And of course my soul is an enemy of God! It and my flesh are buddies, if I'm not careful to feed my spirit (which longs for God and wants only to commune with Him) then those other two will win and I'll become that carnal Christian who is closer to hell than they know. *Let this mind be in me which was also in Christ Jesus!* Phil.2:5 paraphrased.

Make it
PERSONAL

The section which we just finished is a weighty one and can stop forward momentum for many . believers. Renewing of the mind must take place as well as crucifying the flesh. In order to be free in this area of your life, sometimes we need accountability partners. If this area is a stronghold in your life; ask Holy Spirit to send you godly mentors who have overcome and gained victory in these areas. The following are some action steps to help guide you to victory.

- Separate yourself from the people, places, things, images, music etc. that keeps you in a defeated place. -remember the spirit is willing but the flesh is weak
- Replace those things that you have deleted from your life with the things of God. The Bible reminds in Philippians 4:8 to dwell on the things that are true, honest, just, pure lovely, and of a good report.
- Cast down the thoughts that come against the knowledge of God - 2 Corinthians 10:5
- Read the Word of God in order to wash yourself and to remind yourself of who He is!

PART 2

Deliverance

Deliverance

In Christianity, Deliverance Ministry refers to groups that perform practices and rituals to cleanse people of demons and evil spirits. This is done in order to address problems manifesting in their life as a result of demonic presences, which have authority to oppress the person. We must understand legalities. Demons have legal rights to enter in and to possess an individual.

God is the righteous judge and as such He holds court in heaven. Always before His face is Satan, the accuser of the brethren. Satan knows the Word of God and he studies us without ceasing to find our unconfessed sin which he presents to the Father in order that judgment be rendered against us.

Deliverance is (n) the action of being rescued or set free. Deliverance is a part of the benefits package which comes with Salvation. Believers can not be possessed by evil spirits because Holy Spirit lives in our spirit; however, demons can reside in the soul (mind, will and emotions) and even cause illnesses and deformities within the body.

As a believer in Christ, undergoing Deliverance periodically is as necessary as breathing. Brand new Christians or baby believers may need the assistance of those who are equipped and trained to lead them into Deliverance. We have discussed up to this point many different spirits that we can fall prey to by either actively practicing sin, living under curses, or due to generational iniquities and strongholds which have attached to our lineage. In all of these instances, the offending spirit must be identified, called out, repented of and then ultimately be cast out. That is Deliverance in a nutshell.

In the case of practicing sin, which thereby opens doors for intruders to come in, one must be renewed in the mind and have the desire to never actively practice that sin again. We must learn to aggressively and actively detest all sin, especially those that we struggle with. The Bible states that if you open that door (after Deliverance has taken place) again, that foul spirit will return and bring his partners with him and the state of that man will be worse than it was previously.

It is important to detest sin. It must make you ill to think of it. You cannot play footsie with Satan and expect to escape unscathed. Deliverance is not shameful, it's necessary and available to all believers.

As your relationship deepens with the Father, it is possible to undergo self-deliverance. Abiding in the secret place of The Most High God will allow the Holy Spirit to help you to discover the places where Deliverance is needed and can be accomplished then and there.

> ## Deliverance
>
> As you delve into Part 2, you will notice that there are several scriptures in each section. They have been strategically placed to help you begin your study of that topic. *The Bible says study to show yourself approved, a workman that needeth not to be ashamed, rightly dividing the word of truth.*

MY JOURNEY TO FREEDOM

I had to acknowledge that there were areas in my life that I could not see victory in. Because I was a true novice in the spiritual realm, I had to quickly learn all of that which I was lacking. Therefore talk of generational iniquities and strongholds had me baffled. Instinctively, I recognized the truth in what I was learning, but had no point of reference in which to come against the forces that were working against the destiny and purpose that God had placed on and in my life.

The weapons of our warfare are not carnal, but mighty through God to the pulling down of strongholds, 2 Cor. 10:4. For we wrestle not with flesh and blood but against principalities, against powers, against the rulers of the darkness of this world, against spiritual wickedness in high places, Ephesians 6:12.

As I embarked on this journey into truth (as defined by The Word of God) and His standards, I began to recognize that as much as I wanted to move past the old me and enter into the newness of Christ, that I was stuck in many different areas of my life. It was simple for me to see the sins of the flesh and to denounce them - those 10 commandment sins: killing, stealing, coveting, lying, sexing, etc.

My battlefield was my heart and the belief system which had been implanted in me and was now a full-grown forest that hindered my forward progress in the Lord. The following is a list of attitudes and beliefs that I needed and still need to confront by seeking deliverance in those areas. Hear me well, deliverance is only the first step, after Deliverance has occurred, then the real work begins on changing the mind through the washing of the Word, and casting down every high thing which exalts itself against God.

- **Mindset of unbelief**: I did not believe that I was worthy to receive God's best in my own life although I ardently believed for others. This results in Sonship issues, i.e. an orphan spirit.
- **Fear of failure**: This fear kept me stagnant even when I knew that God told me to step out and to perform an action that would bring prosperity/success in my own life. This is a result of brokenness.
- **Remaining in a place of comfort**: for me this was two-fold, I loved comfort, and I was lazy. My God, forgive me! This too, is a result of brokenness.
- **Unyielded to the stretching**: I did not want to go through processes that were designed to take me to the next level, therefore; I was rebellious and stubborn, seeking to make my situation move in the way that I thought that it should. This is a result of brokenness.
- **People-pleasing**: that deep-seated rejection and pride had me looking for the approval of others, rather than seeking the approval of God. I looked up to my leaders so much that I felt that their approval of me was like God saying that He was pleased with me. This too, is a result of brokenness.
- **Inability to confront**: Due to my flawed emotional responses, caused by the strife which I witnessed during my formative years, I had no desire to "fight, argue, reason with" or otherwise engage in conversations which I felt would lead to any unpleasantness. This of course, is counterproductive and results from brokenness.

- **I needed freedom in my mind**: I have since come to the realization that my greatest enemy is the inner me. Whatever I decide not to confront and pull down, will remain. Whatever walls and empty places of the heart that I have established, no matter the reason, will remain until I take up the fight for my life!

The Bible says to let this mind be in me which was also in Christ Jesus. Deliverance is accomplished when you have renewed your mind.

Make it PERSONAL

1. Get a journal, date it and make a list of areas in your life where there is no movement - financially, spiritually, health issues etc. If you do not know how to administer self-deliverance, seek wise and trusted leaders to help you in these areas. After you have undergone Deliverance find scriptures which will help you to obtain victory in remaining and maintaining your freedom.

2. Write them here.

Wisdom is defined as the quality of having experience, knowledge, and good judgment; the quality of being wise.

Wise is defined as having or showing experience, knowledge, and good judgment, <u>marked by deep understanding, keen discernment, and a capacity for sound judgment.</u>

In the book of 1 Kings, Solomon ponders on the question that the Lord asked, *"What should I give you?"* and understands that he needs wisdom above all things to carry out the monumental task of leading and judging Israel.

I Cor.1:24-25 KJV *But unto them which are called, both Jews and Greeks, Christ the power of God, and the wisdom of God.25 Because the foolishness of God is wiser than men; and the weakness of God is stronger than men.*

Prov.3:15 KJV *She is more precious than rubies: and all the things thou canst desire are not to be compared unto her.*

Prov.4:6 KJV *Forsake her not, and she shall preserve thee: love her, and she shall keep thee.*

Proverbs 4:8 (KJV) *Exalt her, and she shall promote thee: she shall bring thee to honour, when thou dost embrace her.*

Proverbs 9:11-12 (KJV) *For by me thy days shall be multiplied, and the years of thy life shall be increased. 12 If thou be wise, thou shalt be wise for thyself: but if thou scornest, thou alone shalt bear it.*

Proverbs 19:8 (KJV) *He that getteth wisdom loveth his own soul: he that keepeth understanding shall find good.*

Proverbs 11:2 (KJV) *When pride cometh, then cometh shame: but with the lowly is wisdom.*

Luke 2:52 (KJV) *And Jesus increased in wisdom and stature, and in favour with God and man.*

James 1:5 (KJV) *If any of you lack wisdom, let him ask of God, that giveth to all men liberally, and upbraideth not; and it shall be given him.*

Ephesians 1:16-17 KJV *Cease not to give thanks for you, making mention of you in my prayers; 17 That the God of our Lord Jesus Christ, the Father of glory, may give unto you the spirit of wisdom and revelation in the knowledge of him:*

Job 12:12 (KJV) *With the ancient is wisdom; and in length of days understanding.*

Psalm 37:30 (KJV) *The mouth of the righteous speaketh wisdom, and his tongue talketh of judgment.*

Proverbs 1:7 (KJV) *The fear of the Lord is the beginning of knowledge: but fools despise wisdom and instruction.*

Proverbs 3:7 (KJV) *Be not wise in thine own eyes: fear the Lord, and depart from evil.*

James 3:17 (KJV) *But the wisdom that is from above is first pure, then peaceable, gentle, and easy to be intreated, full of mercy and good fruits, without partiality, and without hypocrisy.*

1 Corinthians 1:30 (KJV) *But of him are ye in Christ Jesus, who of God is made unto us wisdom, and righteousness, and sanctification, and redemption:*

Proverbs 14:1 (KJV) *Every wise woman buildeth her house: but the foolish plucketh it down with her hands.*

Proverbs 19:20 (KJV) *Hear counsel, and receive instruction, that thou mayest be wise in thy latter end.*

I lacked a deep understanding of issues and situations, had zero discernment and absolutely no capacity for sound judgment. I operated in foolishness, through my trust in my own opinion and flawed logic. *Be not wise in thy own eyes: fear the Lord, and depart from evil.* **Proverbs 3:7 KJV** God's Word has everything that we need for life and health if we would only read and heed it!

In my life as a youngster and well into adulthood, I made horrible, foolish decisions and choices time after time because I lacked wisdom and yielded to my own understanding. I lived according to my responses to emotions and under the bondage of pride, instead of seeking wise counsel. I recall after High School, I received an academic scholarship to UT Knoxville and because of fear and foolish thinking, failed to seek wise counsel, and forfeited what could have been a great blessing in my life. As an older teen, I took part in dangerous sexual practices, engaging in sex without protection. My brokenness led me into making ever more foolish decisions. It didn't stop there, I chose my husband and endured some of the hardest and most painful years of my life. I have come to understand that pride is an adversary of Wisdom. *Wisdom cries out in the street; she raises her voice in the public squares.* Prov. 1:20 ISV.

Make it PERSONAL

1. Are my choices sound? If not, what tools do you use to help you to make decisions? Who has my ear?

2. Is this a generational problem in your family? If so, can you list some poor choices that were made by those close to you (parents, guardians, siblings).

3. Do I seek the Lord before I make major decisions about my life?

Justice

Justice is defined as the quality of being fair and reasonable; the quality of being impartial or fair, the principle or ideal of just dealing or right action. Justice and righteousness walk hand in hand. Justice is a result of righteous living and is a reward to those who live their lives submitted to the will of God and humbled under His mighty hand. In the Kingdom of God, Justice has its roots in the very nature and character of God. He is eternally just; He is Justice. The Bible tells us to enter into His Courts with praise, as a novice I only regarded the definition of courts as a royal place but not as a seat of justice. God is our righteous Judge, He will judge both the quick and the dead. No one can escape the Judgement of God. The believer (under the law) seeks for justice but is condemned by it. Here we find the need for Mercy. The adversary knows the Word of God and uses this knowledge to accuse us before the Father and seek divine judgment. Now behold the Lamb of God! He stands as our advocate and intercedes for us with His precious Blood which speaks for us!

Ecclesiastes 3:17(KJV) *I said in mine heart, God shall judge the righteous and the wicked: for there is a time for every purpose and for every work.*

Hebrews 10:30 (KJV) *For we know him that hath said, Vengeance belongeth unto me, I will recompense, saith the Lord. And again, The Lord shall judge his people.*

Hosea 12:6 (KJV) *Therefore turn thou to thy God: keep mercy and judgment and wait on thy God continually.*

Job 12:22 (KJV) *He discovereth deep things out of darkness, and bringeth out to light the shadow of death.*

Proverbs 21:15 (KJV) *It is joy to the just to do judgment: but destruction shall be to the workers of iniquity.*

Proverbs 24:24-25 (KJV) *He that saith unto the wicked, Thou are righteous; him shall the people curse, nations shall abhor him: 25 But to them that rebuke him shall be delight, and a good blessing shall come upon them.*

Proverbs 28:5 (KJV) *Evil men understand not judgment: but they that seek the Lord understand all things.*

Matthew 5:38-39 (KJV) *Ye have heard that it hath been said, An eye for an eye, and a tooth for a tooth: 39 But I say unto you, That ye resist not evil: but whosoever shall smite thee on thy right cheek, turn to him the other also.*

Amos 5:24(KJV) *But let judgment run down as waters, and righteousness as a mighty stream.*

Psalm 37:27-29 (KJV) *27 Depart from evil, and do good; and dwell for evermore. 28 For the Lord loveth judgment, and forsaketh not his saints; they are preserved for ever: but the seed of the wicked shall be cut off. 29 The righteous shall inherit the land, and dwell therein forever.*

Romans 12:19 (KJV) *Dearly beloved, avenge not yourselves, but rather give place unto wrath: for it is written, Vengeance is mine; I will repay, saith the Lord.*

    I can remember always believing that fairness alluded my life even as a young child. I felt as if all around me, other people, had things, did things and basically lived the life that I desperately wished for. I remember eventually thinking that justice would never be a part of my life because so many events transpired that left me feeling like I would always be the underdog.

    My family's financial status never seemed to improve although my daddy worked long hours and even over the road as a truck driver. I distinctly recall in Jr. High School, how my peers made fun of me for my lack of trendy clothes and shoes, and my nappy hair that was never quite up to the standards of that time. One of the most hurtful instances of injustice was one Sunday morning when I was probably 16. I ate a bowl of cereal and for some reason I vomited and my father accused me of being pregnant. It's ironic that at that time I was too afraid to have sex, but that indictment would prove true three years later when the words that he spoke against me came to pass.

Make it PERSONAL

1. How do you feel about the death penalty? Do your thoughts line up with the nature and character of God? Give proof.

2. Do you judge others unfairly? Do you use a double standard when making judgment calls? Why?

Holiness

Holiness: the state of being holy. Holy: dedicated or consecrated to God or a religious purpose; sacred. Sanctification: the state of growing in divine grace as a result of Christian commitment after baptism or conversion. Holiness is the goal in living a life that is set apart for God's purpose and calling. After conversion, God begins the process of establishing a holy mindset in the believer. Because we are new creations in Christ, we have taken on the identity of a son of God. Sons are like their fathers in appearance, actions, and mindsets. God requires Holiness in order to complete His work in our lives. So holiness is not an idea, but a way of life - a requirement in order to do the work of the Kingdom. We have thrown shame on God's great name by professing a holiness that we do not demonstrate on a daily basis.

I was taught by example to say one thing and to do something else completely. I witnessed inappropriate relationships between authority figures and children. The exchange of money, clothes, food and favors for sexual acts. All the while, Holiness was preached from the pulpit; but the congregation, top-down, was anything but. Sexual immorality was prevalent; there were more people engaged in illicit relationships than those who were not. The concept of a holy and righteous marriage seemed to be an abstract that could only be achieved by couples almost at death's door. Yet, the Word was preached without any conviction or manifestation. There were very few righteous role models for marriage at church, and of course there was the unsettling marriage that I witnessed in my home. Due to what I witnessed in my formative years, I took on the mindset of do what you feel. This has been extremely damaging in my life. My belief in God coupled with a lack of holiness led me to some very dark and desperate places, both in the physical and spiritual. It caused me to deaden my heart to what Holy Spirit wanted for me and from me. My life was like a seesaw with high highs and damaging lows. As 2 Cor. 7:1 says I needed to cleanse myself from ALL filthiness of the flesh and spirit. I am so grateful that God had mercy on me and allowed me to experience the truth of His Word!

2 Corinthians 7:1 (KJV) *Having therefore these promises, dearly beloved, let us cleanse ourselves from all filthiness of the flesh and spirit, perfecting holiness in the fear of God*

1 Peter 1:15-16 (KJV) *But as he which hath called you is holy, so be ye holy in all manner of conversation; 16 Because it is written, Be ye holy; for I am holy.*

Hebrews 12:14 (KJV) *Follow peace with all men, and holiness, without which no man shall see the Lord:*

Psalm 119:9 (KJV) *Wherewithal shall a young man cleanse his way? by taking heed thereto according to thy word.*

2 Timothy 1:9 (KJV) *Who hath saved us, and called us with an holy calling, not according to our works, but according to his own purpose and grace, which was given us in Christ Jesus before the world began,*

Psalm 139:23-24 (KJV) *Search me, O God, and know my heart: try me, and know my thoughts: 24 And see if there be any wicked way in me, and lead me in the way everlasting.*

Philippians 2:5 (KJV) *Let this mind be in you, which was also in Christ Jesus:*

Philippians 2:14-16 (KJV) *Do all things without murmurings and disputings:15 That ye may be blameless and harmless, the sons of God, without rebuke, in the midst of a crooked and perverse nation, among whom ye shine as lights in the world;16 Holding forth the word of life; that I may rejoice in the day of Christ, that I have not run in vain, neither laboured in vain.*

Ephesians 5:3 (KJV) *But fornication, and all uncleanness, or covetousness, let it not be once named among you, as becometh saints;*

Romans 12:1(KJV) *I beseech you therefore, brethren, by the mercies of God, that ye present your bodies a living sacrifice, holy, acceptable unto God, which is your reasonable service.*

1 Samuel 2:2 (KJV) *There is none holy as the Lord: for there is none beside thee: neither is there any rock like our God.*

Isaiah 57:15 (KJV) *For thus saith the high and lofty One that inhabiteth eternity, whose name is Holy; I dwell in the high and holy place, with him also that is of a contrite and humble spirit, to revive the spirit of the humble, and to revive the heart of the contrite ones*

Leviticus 20:26(KJV) *And ye shall be holy unto me: for I the Lord am holy, and have severed you from other people, that ye should be mine.*

Make it PERSONAL

1. Do you place Holiness above everything else in your life? List some areas in your life where your holiness could be called into question.

2. Do you suffer from the mindset that it is impossible to achieve the righteous standard that God requires? Why do you feel this way? Are you taking up your cross daily and dying to the flesh?

PART 3

Righteousness\Sanctification

Righteousness / Sanctification

Righteousness: the quality of being morally right or justifiable, acting in accord with divine or moral law; free from guilt or sin. The phrase in the definition, "the quality of" means a certain value. This term righteousness, as defined by the God of the universe, leaves us(mankind) completely lacking. *He says that in our flesh dwells no good thing* (Romans 7:18 NKJV) *and that our righteousness is as filthy rags in his eyesight.* (Isaiah 64:6 KJV) paraphrase.

To be honest, the term righteousness, to most individuals, let alone believers, is a daunting one. I think (as people) we possess a deep instinctual understanding of our true unworthiness to stand before a completely Holy and Righteous God. This understanding, coupled with an incomplete/erroneous knowledge of the Word of God and His nature leaves many doubting their ability to be anything other than fallen, thereby perpetuating a spirit of Godlessness in our lives. This gives rise to a religious spirit that comes up with cliches and old wives tales regarding man's heart and his ability (or most often inability) to live as God has declared that we should as His children.

God's Word is so powerful (mighty, strong, invincible) and is able to wash and cleanse , and to keep us; so the enemy does everything in his power to keep us from reading, understanding, meditating and being freed by It. We must become self feeders of the Word of God! When we seek Him with our whole hearts, He will open up the treasure of His Word to us. Righteousness is simple, as are all of the things of God. We must first submit our wills underneath His will and begin to grow as we turn away from the sin and the weight that it brings. In order to be Righteous, I must first be sanctified.

Sanctification speaks to the act of being set apart. If I do not actively, consciously and intentionally set myself apart, I will not achieve the righteous state that God is requiring of me. There are some processes and journeys that must be observed, adhered to, and undertaken in order to reach our full potential in Christ. We often put these spooky spiritual connotations on the precepts of God, when Jesus

Himself, during His earthly ministry, made every teaching as plain as possible. For example, I have some clothing that I only wear on specific occasions, therefore, I can say that those items are sanctified, they are set apart. Now, when we speak on God and sanctification, let's use that same definition. I will actively, consciously, and intentionally set myself apart for His Glory and for His Use and for His Purpose! This simply means that I make up my mind to do the will of the Father, come hell or high water. Just as those items of clothing are not for ordinary use or everyday wear, my life is now fully committed to God and is NOT for partaking in the common (sinful, unrighteous, unGodly) activities that I participated in before I received the precious gift of Salvation.

Psalm 85:10 (KJV) *Mercy and truth are met together; righteousness and peace have kissed each other.*

Psalm 1:6 (KJV) *For the Lord knoweth the way of the righteous: but the way of the ungodly shall perish.*

Psalm 5:12 (KJV) *For thou, Lord, wilt bless the righteous; with favour wilt thou compass him as with a shield.*

Psalm 23:3 (KJV) *He restoreth my soul: he leadeth me in the paths of righteousness for his name's sake.*

Psalm 7:9 (KJV) *Oh let the wickedness of the wicked come to an end; but establish the just: for the righteous God trieth the hearts and reins.*

Psalm 9:8 (KJV) *And he shall judge the world in righteousness, he shall minister judgment to the people in uprightness.*

Psalm 28:1 (KJV) *Unto thee will I cry, O Lord my rock; be not silent to me: lest, if thou be silent to me, I become like them that go down into the pit.*

Psalm 145:17 (KJV) *The Lord is righteous in all his ways, and holy in all his works.*

Psalm 118:19 (KJV) *Open to me the gates of righteousness: I will go into them, and I will praise the Lord:*

Proverbs 11:19 (KJV) *As righteousness tendeth to life: so he that pursueth evil pursueth it to his own death.*

Proverbs 11:5 (KJV) *The righteousness of the perfect shall direct his way: but the wicked shall fall by his own wickedness.*

Isaiah 32:17 (KJV) *And the work of righteousness shall be peace; and the effect of righteousness quietness and assurance forever.*

Isaiah 64:6 (KJV) *But we are all as an unclean thing, and all our righteousnesses are as filthy rags; and we all do fade as a leaf; and our iniquities, like the wind, have taken us away.*

THE STRUGGLE IS REAL

My family began to attend church regularly the year that I turned twelve, where before, we attended church once a year on Easter Sunday. Unfortunately, I learned how to be hypocritical and people-pleasing almost from the beginning. I was an excellent "performer". I learned how to gauge the crowd and to use my intellect and legalistic knowledge of scripture to provide comments that would insure a favorable response. Can both fresh water and salt water flow from the same spring? In the sanctuary and classroom, I was an angel, but in the parking lot I was foul-mouthed and fast, seeking to fit in with my peers.

During my youth, I was never called out for my wicked behavior. It was overlooked and caused me to never be held accountable for living with one foot precariously in the Kingdom of Light and the other firmly planted in the Kingdom of Darkness. The strange thing was, I loved Jesus but didn't know Him. How can this be? Righteousness must become your way of life, so that you may be sanctified for His use. As a matter of fact, setting your life apart for His use will allow Him to plant the seed of righteousness in your life. Consider the parable of the sower, he goes out and sows his seed and it scatters to different types of soil. What type of heart (soil) do you possess? Is it able to receive the seed and yield an abundant harvest?

Make it PERSONAL

1. As a believer, how important is it to you to uphold the righteous standard?

2. Will you bend under pressure and accept what God is against or will you cry loud and spare not?

3. Are there certain groups of people that you tend to feel are above God's law?

Fruit of the Spirit

The Fruit of the Spirit is maintained or grown by living a fasted lifestyle, while being immersed in the Word of God and dwelling in the presence of the Lord. We must not forsake the process that God has for us to grow and become who He wants us to be. Each fruit of the Spirit grows at a different pace and each is unique to the individual. The greatest of these is love, and we are to seek love above all others. None of the other fruit will grow without the presence of love.

To attain love, you must ask the Father to reveal His heart for people to you. We cannot operate in love without understanding the weight and the depth of the Father's love for us and having the understanding that we are not worthy of His love due to any efforts of our own. We are also to seek wisdom. Wisdom cries from the streets and is there to help us as we navigate this life. We must also cultivate an intimate relationship with the Father. It's also important to know that our love walk will be tested. James 1:2-4. Once again, don't rush the process, during the time that you are building/growing/obtaining the Fruit of the Spirit, God has you on His wheel and He is refining you and making you into His image and likeness. Read Galatians 5:22-23 and do a deep dive on the Fruit of the Spirit. Be honest and determine if they live in your heart and our tangible in your life.

Galatians 5:22-23 (KJV) *But the fruit of the Spirit is love, joy, peace, longsuffering, gentleness, goodness, faith, 23 Meekness, temperance: against such there is no law.*

Love

1st John, 4th chapter speaks on how to discern spirits, The Spirit of God, the spirit of man and unclean spirits. If a person preaches Jesus Christ as Lord and Savior, then that person is of God. That person will hate the world (carnality) and love what God loves (light, wholeness, truth). It also determines how to know if you possess the love of God. According to v.13 (we will have His Spirit) & v.15 - we will confess and profess Jesus as the Son of God. True love stems from possessing the heart of God - feeling the weight of His love and the depth of his compassion. Our heart's cry should be for the Father to show us His heart. True love.

Ephesians 3:16-17 (KJV) *That he would grant you, according to the riches of his glory, to be strengthened with might by his Spirit in the inner man;17 That Christ may dwell in your hearts by faith; that ye, being rooted and grounded in love,*

1 John 4:16 (KJV) *And we have known and believed the ove that God hath to us. God is love; and he that dwelleth in love dwelleth in God, and God in him.*

1 Corinthians 13:4-8 (KJV) *Charity suffereth long, and is kind; charity envieth not; charity vaunteth not itself, is not puffed up, 5 Doth not behave itself unseemly, seeketh not her own, is not easily provoked, thinketh no evil; 6 Rejoiceth not in iniquity, but rejoiceth in the truth; 7 Beareth all things, believeth all things, hopeth all things, endureth all things. 8 Charity never faileth: but whether there be prophecies, they shall fail; whether there be tongues, they shall cease; whether there be knowledge, it shall*

Make it PERSONAL

1. Do you possess God's heart in the way that he views His creation and His children? Are you a respecter of persons?

2. 1 Cor. 13:4-8 talks about what love does and does not do? Make a list and rate yourself on a scale of 1-10. Where do you stand?

noun a feeling of great pleasure and happiness

Jesus is the source of True Joy. This joy can only be found in our Lord & Savior Jesus Christ. His sacrificial action ensured that we would be presented to the Father, wherein there is fullness of joy!

Over is an adverb that describes how believers should posture their lives when it comes to the tricks and the wiles of the enemy. In our overcoming, there is joy because of the strength of the Undefeated One, the Lord Jesus Christ!

You, meaning me, are the embodiment of my and your life as a sinful fallen man. This fleshly carnal nature can in no way stand in the presence of a Holy & Righteous God. Man must have a Savior; I must have a Savior. Thank you Jesus. Joy equals strength. Without joy , we have no power, there is no way that we can walk in peace and love without joy. Joy demands that we view our lives through the blood of Jesus and his ultimate sacrifice which ushers us into a joy that is inconceivable even in the midst of life's trials and tribulations.

Jesus Over Yourself

Ephesians 2:1-2 NLT Once you were dead because of your disobedience and your many sins. 2 You used to live in sin, just like the rest of the world, obeying the devil—the commander of the powers in the unseen world. He is the spirit at work in the hearts of those who refuse to obey God.

Galatians 5:19-21 The Message 19-21 It is obvious what kind of life develops out of trying to get your own way all the time: repetitive, loveless, cheap sex; a stinking accumulation of mental and emotional garbage; frenzied and joyless grabs for happiness; trinket gods; magic-show religion; paranoid loneliness; cutthroat competition; all-consuming-yet-never-satisfied wants; a brutal temper; an impotence to love or be loved; divided homes and divided lives; small-minded and lopsided pursuits; the vicious habit of depersonalizing everyone into a rival; uncontrolled and uncontrollable addictions; ugly parodies of community. I could go on. This isn't the first time I have warned you, you know. If you use your freedom this way, you will not inherit God's kingdom.

Romans 7:18 (KJV) For I know that in me (that is, in my flesh,) dwelleth no good thing: for to will is present with me; but how to perform that which is good I find not.

Hebrews 12:2 (KJV) Looking unto Jesus the author and finisher of our faith; who for the joy that was set before him endured the cross, despising the shame, and is set down at the right hand of the throne of God.

Nehemiah 8:10 (KJV) *Then he said unto them, Go your way, eat the fat, and drink the sweet, and send portions unto them for whom nothing is prepared: for this day is holy unto our Lord: neither be ye sorry; for the joy of the Lord is your strength.*

Romans 15:13 (KJV) *Now the God of hope fill you with all joy and peace in believing, that ye may abound in hope, through the power of the Holy Ghost.*

Colossians 1:11 (KJV) *Strengthened with all might, according to his glorious power, unto all patience and longsuffering with joyfulness;*

Make it
PERSONAL

1. The Word says that the joy of the Lord is our strength; how do you maintain His joy in your life?

2. Write about a time when His joy was elusive to you. What did you do?

Jehovah Shalom (The Lord is Peace)

*Peace is defined as the freedom from disturbance, tranquility. 2 Tranquility, calm, calmness, to **be complete/sound, peace, the absence from strife.***

Peace is more valuable than any commodity known to mankind. Man has struggled to find peace of mind during times of duress and even in times of plenty. It is ironic to note that in the natural, as far as possessions are concerned, the poorest person and the wealthiest individual can experience a lack of peace. Peace can not be bought, bargained for or bartered. True and lasting peace, the peace that surpasses all understanding, all circumstances, all life events, death events come from Abba Father. His peace is unexplainable, unmerited and freely given to His children. He shall keep your mind in perfect peace, when you keep your mind on Him.

Just recently, I experienced the passing of my son-in-law and my father. Throughout the entire process of saying farewell, I existed in a state of peace that I could not explain. Any anxiety that I experienced, came when "I" attempted to carry the burden myself. The Bible says to cast your cares upon Him because He cares for you. It also says that His yoke is easy and His burdens are light. The absence of peace comes when there is an absence of Jesus.

Romans 5:1 (KJV) Therefore being justified by faith, we have peace with God through our Lord Jesus Christ:

Judges 6:24 KJV Then Gideon built an altar there unto the Lord, and called it Jehovah-shalom: unto this day it is yet in Ophrah of the Abi-ezrites.

Philippians 4:6-7,9 KJV Be careful for nothing; but in every thing by prayer and supplication with thanksgiving let your requests be made known unto God. [7] And the peace of God, which passeth all understanding, shall keep your hearts and minds through Christ Jesus. [9] Those things, which ye have both learned, and received, and heard, and seen in me, do: and the God of peace shall be with you.

Psalm 4:8 KJV I will both lay me down in peace, and sleep: for thou, Lord, only makest me dwell in safety.

1 Peter 3:11 KJV Let him eschew evil, and do good; let him seek peace, and ensue it.

Isaiah 26:3 KJV Thou wilt keep him in perfect peace, whose mind is stayed on thee : because he trusteth in thee.

1 Thessalonians 5:23 KJV And the very God of peace sanctify you wholly; and I pray God your whole spirit and soul and body be preserved blameless unto the coming of our Lord Jesus Christ.

John 14:27 KJV Peace I leave with you, my peace I give unto you: not as the world giveth, give I unto you. Let not your heart be troubled, neither let it be afraid.

Matthew 5:9 KJV Blessed are the peacemakers: for they shall be called the children of God.

Colossians 3:15 KJV And let the peace of God rule in your hearts, to the which also ye are called in one body; and be ye thankful.

Make it
PERSONAL

1. How important is peace to you? Have you ever intentionally caused someone else to lose their peace?

2. Would you rather have peace than financial prosperity? What's the correlation?

Patience

1. the capacity to accept or tolerate delay, trouble, or suffering without getting angry or upset 2. the level of endurance one can have before disrespect

Patience is a virtue. This is an old saying but most definitely a true one. The virtue of possessing patience is huge! God demonstrates to us how patience should look as He deals with us, His children on a daily basis. As the Father demonstrates to us, we should demonstrate to others. Possessing patience builds the ability to endure long suffering. If one does not possess patience, then longsuffering is a fruit that will barely be achieved. God wants us to look like His only begotten Son, Jesus, who personified everything that The Father adores. He withstood insolence , unbelief, disrespect, and so many other insults. Our lives must mirror Jesus' life! One must have a quiet spirit that is open to peace in order to achieve patience. Thank you Jesus for your patience and love towards us! Spend some time meditating on the following scriptures during your personal devotional time.

Ecclesiastes 7:8 KJV Better is the end of a thing than the beginning thereof: and the patient in spirit is better than the proud in spirit.

James 5:8 KJV Be ye also patient; stablish your hearts: for the coming of the Lord draweth nigh.

Romans 12:12 KJV Rejoicing in hope; patient in tribulation; continuing instant in prayer;

Psalm 40:1 KJV I waited patiently for the Lord ; and he inclined unto me, and heard my cry.

Romans 8:25 KJV But if we hope for that we see not, then do we with patience wait for it.

Galatians 6:9 KJV And let us not be weary in well doing: for in due season we shall reap, if we faint not.

Colossians 3:12 KJV Put on therefore, as the elect of God, holy and beloved, bowels of mercies, kindness, humbleness of mind, meekness, longsuffering;

Romans 15:5 KJV Now the God of patience and consolation grant you to be like minded one toward another according to Christ Jesus:

2 Peter 3:8 KJV But, beloved, be not ignorant of this one thing, that one day is with the Lord as a thousand years, and a thousand years as one day.

Hebrews 10:36 KJV For ye have need of patience, that, after ye have done the will of God, ye might receive the promise.

Lamentations 3:25-26 KJV The Lord is good unto them that wait for him, to the soul that seeketh him. 26 It is good that a man should both hope and quietly wait for the salvation of the Lord.

Psalm 37:7 KJV Rest in the Lord, and wait patiently for him: fret not thyself because of him who prospereth in his way, because of the man who bringeth wicked devices to pass.

Make it PERSONAL

1. Have you learned how to wait patiently on the Lord? Do you struggle with times and seasons?

2. Where/when do you struggle the most in regards to patience

Faithfulness

Great is your faithfulness to me, morning by morning, new mercies I see. Oh great is Your faithfulness to me!

Once again when thinking about this fruit of the Spirit, I am reminded of the oh so great faithfulness of God. I am also brought into remembrance of the great faith heroes in the Word. In Hebrews, Chapter 11, we are directed back to the lives of Abraham, Moses, Abel, Enoch, Noah, Sara etc. They all were counted faithful by God. Now faith is the substance of things hoped for, the evidence of things not seen. God respects, requires and rewards faithfulness in His children. We as people appreciate and respect when faithfulness is demonstrated in relationships, family ties, jobs and organizations.

Faithfulness has become a thing of the past as people spend time looking after their own interests and desires, often shirking commitments to both God and man. Faith is the currency we exchange with heaven. Our faith demonstrates our trust in God - indeed how much in fact we do trust in Him. 2 Corinthians 3:18…but we all, with unveiled face, beholding as in a mirror the glory of the Lord, are being transformed into the same image from glory to glory , just as by the spirit of the Lord. The Bible says in Romans 1:17, *for in it the righteousness of God is revealed from faith to faith. As it is written, "The just shall live by faith."* Finally, Romans 10:17 says *so then faith comes by hearing , and hearing by the Word of God.*

Look at the following passages of scripture and identify at least two to commit to memory.

Matthew 17:20 KJV And Jesus said unto them, Because of your unbelief: for verily I say unto you, If ye have faith as a grain of mustard seed, ye shall say unto this mountain, Remove hence to yonder place; and it shall remove; and nothing shall be impossible unto you.

Romans 5:1-2 KJV Therefore being justified by faith, we have peace with God through our Lord Jesus Christ: 2 By whom also we have access by faith into this grace wherein we stand, and rejoice in hope of the glory of God.

Romans 10:8-11 KJV But what saith it? The word is nigh thee, even in thy mouth, and in thy heart: that is, the word of faith, which we preach; 9 That if thou shalt confess with thy mouth the Lord Jesus, and shalt believe in thine heart that God hath raised him from the dead, thou shalt be saved. 10 For with the heart man believeth unto righteousness; and with the mouth confession is made unto salvation. 11 For the scripture saith, Whosoever believeth on him shall not be ashamed.

Mark 11:22-25 KJV And Jesus answering saith unto them, Have faith in God. 23 For verily I say unto you, That whosoever shall say unto this mountain, Be thou removed, and be thou cast into the sea; and shall not doubt in his heart, but shall believe that those things which he saith shall come to pass; he shall have whatsoever he saith. 24 Therefore I say unto you, What things soever ye desire, when ye pray, believe that ye receive them, and ye shall have them. 25 And when ye stand praying, forgive, if ye have ought against any: that your Father also which is in heaven may forgive you your trespasses.

Romans 1:17 KJV For therein is the righteousness of God revealed from faith to faith: as it is written, The just shall live by faith.

1 Peter 1:6-9 KJV Wherein ye greatly rejoice, though now for a season, if need be, ye are in heaviness through manifold temptations: 7 That the trial of your faith, being much more precious than of gold that perisheth, though it be tried with fire, might be found unto praise and honour and glory at the appearing of Jesus Christ: 8 Whom having not seen, ye love; in whom, though now ye see him not, yet believing, ye rejoice with joy unspeakable and full of glory: 9 Receiving the end of your faith, even the salvation of your souls.

Ephesians 2:8-9 KJV For by grace are ye saved through faith; and that not of yourselves: it is the gift of God:9 Not of works, lest any man should boast.

Hebrews 11:1-6 KJV Now faith is the substance of things hoped for, the evidence of things not seen. 2 For by it the elders obtained a good report. 3 Through faith we understand that the worlds were framed by the word of God, so that things which are seen were not made of things which do appear. 4 By faith Abel offered unto God a more excellent sacrifice than Cain, by which he obtained witness that he was righteous, God testifying of his gifts: and by it he being dead yet speaketh. 5 By faith Enoch was translated that he should not see death; and was not found, because God had translated him: for before his translation he had this testimony, that he pleased God. 6 But without faith it is impossible to please him : for he that cometh to God must believe that he is, and that he is a rewarder of them that diligently seek him.

Make it PERSONAL

1. Where are you in your faith walk?

2. Does your faith show up in your commitments to God and to others?

3. List some areas where you have seen your faith produce results.

4. How can you replicate that same success in other areas of your life?

Longsuffering

---

adjective: **longsuffering having or showing patience in spite of troubles, especially those caused by other people. patient, forbearing, tolerant, uncomplaining,**

In order to become a true convert to Christ, one needs to develop the **fruit** of long suffering. This requires a level of spiritual maturity which many (for whatever reason) do not achieve/attain. Having the mind of Christ, "let this mind be in me which was also in Christ Jesus- means that you carry the thoughts, mindset, and personality of the Father. Jesus said, "I only say what my Father says and I only do what my Father does." Likewise, as we grow more into the image of Christ, we will learn how to labor long (in a spirit of love) with people, those who are for us, as well as those who are against us.

Jesus and His interactions with the 12 disciples are a prime example. Jesus spent three years with these men; teaching, exhorting, discipling, loving and rebuking them. He did not make a difference between the 11 and the 1 (Judas Iscariot) who would betray him. We must develop this fruit in order to bring glory to God and make His Name great! I have struggled with this fruit all of my Christian life. I now understand that my lack of obedience in this area has led me into a wilderness episode. There have been so many tests of my character which I have failed because of dwelling in my emotions and a stubborn refusal to give grace, patience, and understanding to those in my life who needed me to dig in and walk them through some tough times. Holy Spirit has been leading me as of late to repent of my impatience and selfishness so that this fruit will grow in my life; after all, it's not about me, but about those to whom I've been called.

1 Corinthians 13:4,7 NIV Love is patient, love is kind. It does not envy, it does not boast, it is not proud. 7 It always protects, always trusts, always hopes, always perseveres.

2 Corinthians 6:4-6 NIV Rather, as servants of God we commend ourselves in every way: in great endurance; in troubles, hardships and distresses; 5 in beatings, imprisonments and riots; in hard work, sleepless nights and hunger; 6 in purity, understanding, patience and kindness; in the Holy Spirit and in sincere love;

Galatians 5:22 But the fruit of the Spirit is love, joy, peace, forbearance, kindness, goodness, faithfulness,

Ephesians 4: 1-2 As a prisoner for the Lord, then, I urge you to live a life worthy of the calling you have received. 2 Be completely humble and gentle; be patient, bearing with one another in love

Colossians 1:11 being strengthened with all power according to his glorious might so that you may have great endurance and patience,

Colossians 3:12-13 Therefore, as God's chosen people, holy and dearly loved, clothe yourselves with compassion, kindness, humility, gentleness and patience. 13 Bear with each other and forgive one another if any of you has a grievance against someone. Forgive as the Lord forgave you.

1 Timothy 1:16 But for that very reason I was shown mercy so that in me, the worst of sinners, Christ Jesus might display his immense patience as an example for those who would believe in him and receive eternal life.

2 Timothy 3:10 You, however, know all about my teaching, my way of life, my purpose, faith, patience, love, endurance,

2 Timothy 4:2 Preach the word; be prepared in season and out of season; correct, rebuke and encourage—with great patience and careful instruction.

Make it PERSONAL

1. What are your thoughts concerning this fruit?

2. Are you willing to go the extra mile with people, or do you tend to throw in the towel?

3. How have your attitudes affected your life and your walk with Christ?

4. List some action steps that will help you to achieve victory in this area.

Goodness

the quality of being morally good or virtuous, virtue, virtuousness good, righteousness, morality, ethicalness

God is good. God = good. Jesus said, "Why callest thou me good? There is none good but God." Jesus said, there is <u>NO ONE</u> good but God. We must redefine our concept of what the terms "good" and "goodness" really mean. We often think of ourselves as being *good citizens, good people, good this or good that.* The word good is defined as that which is morally right; righteousness. We, by our very nature, can never be described as good. We possess, before salvation, a sin nature.

This goes back to the fall of man, Adam & Eve in the Garden of Eden. We can not even have a sense of morality without the very existence of God. He had to tell us what was good/right or bad/wrong i.e. the Ten Commandments. The further away man went from the Garden where there was fellowship with God, the deeper the chasm grew between God and man. **Genesis 6:5 GWT,** *The LORD was sorry that he had made humans on the earth, and he was heartbroken.* The GWT says that our Father was heartbroken. The Bible speaks of goodness around 50 times and each reference pertains to God and how He will grant goodness, allow goodness, give goodness to us. We praise God for His goodness that He extends to us and through the sacrifice of Jesus we are able to carry goodness as well! Thank you Jesus for your victory which is our victory! Glory!!

Psalm 107:9 KJV For he satisfieth the longing soul, and filleth the hungry soul with goodness.

Romans 2:4 KJV Or despisest thou the riches of his goodness and forbearance and longsuffering; not knowing that the goodness of God leadeth thee to repentance?

Psalm 136:1-3 KJV O give thanks unto the Lord ; for he is good: for his mercy endureth forever. 2 O give thanks unto the God of gods: for his mercy endureth for ever. 3 O give thanks to the Lord of lords: for his mercy endureth for ever.

Lamentations 3:22-26 KJV It is of the Lord's mercies that we are not consumed, because his compassions fail not. 23 They are new every morning: great is thy faithfulness. 24 The Lord is my portion, saith my soul; therefore will I hope in him. 25 The Lord is good unto them that wait for him, to the soul that seeketh him. 26 It is good that a man should both hope and quietly wait for the salvation of the Lord.

Mark 10:18 KJV And Jesus said unto him, Why callest thou me good? there is none good but one, that is, God.

James 1:17 KJV Every good gift and every perfect gift is from above, and cometh down from the Father of lights, with whom is no variableness, neither shadow of turning.

1 Chronicles 16:34 KJV O give thanks unto the Lord ; for he is good; for his mercy endureth forever.

Make it PERSONAL

1. Can you identify any areas of your life that you know are lacking in Goodness?

2. List them and ask Holy Spirit's help to develop this fruit in your life.

Meekness & Gentleness

Meekness - noun *the fact or condition of being meek; submissiveness. patience, long-suffering, forbearance, resignation, gentleness*

Gentleness noun **1. the quality of being kind, tender, or** *mild-mannered. kindness, kindliness, tenderness, benignity*

Galatians 6:1 (KJV) *Brethren, if a man be overtaken in a fault, ye which are spiritual, restore such a one in the spirit of meekness; considering thyself, lest thou also be tempted.*

2 Peter 1:5-7 (KJV) *And beside this, giving all diligence, add to your faith virtue; and to virtue knowledge; 6 And to knowledge temperance; and to temperance patience; and to patience godliness; 7 And to godliness brotherly kindness; and to brotherly kindness charity.*

I have included Meekness and Gentleness under the same heading because the two compliment each other so well, and when discussing the fruit of the spirit, they are hard to separate. When I consider what meekness looks like, I think about bowed heads, subdued tongues, exchanging the right for the wrong, taking the Loss when Winning is our right. Meekness is NOT weakness. Meekness is power under control. Meekness says that I have the ability and the discipline to control myself. Not by might, not by power, but by the Spirit of The Most High God! The Bible says that Jesus was meek and lowly, but we know that He is (as my Prophetess Felecia Wade often says) the strongest, strongest One! His meekness made the cross possible. His meekness led to yours and my salvation. His meekness led to the salvation of the world without end! He is our brother, our High Priest, our Chief Intercessor, our Sovereign Lord. He is our mentor and we are to BE LIKE HIM! In order to endure persecution, trials, suffering and death will take a level of Meekness forged through the death of the flesh! We must be led by the Spirit and not walk after the flesh.

Galatians 5:22 GW But the spiritual nature produces love, joy, peace, patience, kindness, goodness, faithfulness

Numbers 12:3 GW (Moses was a very humble man, more humble than anyone else on earth.)

Romans 12:14 KJV Bless them which persecute you: bless, and curse not.

1 Peter 3:4,15 KJV But let it be the hidden man of the heart, in that which is not corruptible, even the ornament of a meek and quiet spirit, which is in the sight of God of great price. [15] But sanctify the Lord God in your hearts: and be ready always to give an answer to every man that asketh you a reason of the hope that is in you with meekness and fear:

James 3:13 KJV Who is a wise man and endued with knowledge among you? let him shew out of a good conversation his works with meekness of wisdom.

Psalm 25:9 KJV The meek will he guide in judgment: and the meek will he teach his way.

Matthew 5:5 KJV Blessed are the meek: for they shall inherit the earth.

Psalm 37:11 KJV But the meek shall inherit the earth; and shall delight themselves in the abundance of peace.

Matthew 11:29 KJV Take my yoke upon you, and learn of me; for I am meek and lowly in heart: and ye shall find rest unto your souls.

Titus 3:2 KJV To speak evil of no man, to be no brawlers, but gentle, shewing all meekness unto all men.

Make it PERSONAL

1. List two personal situations in which Meekness and Gentleness would have made the difference in a confrontation/situation.

2. Rewrite those scenarios with a different outcome- what would/could have happened if I had approached it as Christ would?

Self-Control

noun **the ability to control oneself, in particular one's emotions and desires or the expression of them in one's behavior, especially in difficult situations. self-discipline, self-**
restraint, restraint, control, self-mastery

It's funny, when I think about this fruit, I am always reminded of the Kindergarten Report Card and one of the chief indicators of being ready to learn reads like this: The ability to maintain self-control. The

Kindergarten grading scale is either an M (mastery) or an X (non-mastery). Either you possess it or you don't.

Self-Control is a fundamental attribute that must be learned and cultivated early in life to insure a certain level of socio-emotional success of the individual. That holds true in the natural, it is equally as relevant in the Spirit realm. 90% of the work of becoming like Christ is rooted in self-control. When the believer understands that their choices will dictate their level of maturity and how fast and or how far they progress in the things of God is directly correlated to their ability to maintain self-control.

The lusts of the flesh, the lust of the eyes and the pride of life (1 John 2:16) are all subject to our own will. The question is simple: Will I choose what God loves or will I choose what edifies my flesh? If I choose the former, then Holy Spirit is more than willing and able to help me to be an overcomer. On the flip side, my unwillingness to mortify my flesh will lead me on the path to destruction. John 3:19 And this is the condemnation, that light is come into the world, and men loved darkness rather than light, because their deeds were evil.

My own struggle with self-control has been an epic one. Sexual sin, pride, envy, covetousness - all have played a part in my life. My love of the darkness, rather than the light, had me in this place. I had to learn that I Can Not Trust My Flesh. It (my flesh) is an enemy of God and my spirit man, who longs to live for God and to be immersed in His presence and His Glory. Through God's grace and mercy, He has helped me to begin to achieve self-control. It is a constant battle, I would be lying to say otherwise, but thanks be to God who gives me the victory.

Galatians 5:22-23 KJV But the fruit of the Spirit is love, joy, peace, longsuffering, gentleness, goodness, faith, 23 Meekness, temperance: against such there is no law.

Romans 7:18 For I know that in me (that is, in my flesh,) dwelleth no good thing: for to will is present with me; but how to perform that which is good I find not.

Proverbs 25: 27-28 It is not good to eat much honey: so for men to search their own glory is not glory. 28 He that hath no rule over his own spirit is like a city that is broken down, and without walls.

1 Corinthians 7:5 5 Defraud ye not one the other, except it be with consent for a time, that ye may give yourselves to fasting and prayer; and come together again, that Satan tempt you not for your incontinency.

1 Timothy 3:2-3 A bishop then must be blameless, the husband of one wife, vigilant, sober, of good behaviour, given to hospitality, apt to teach; 3 Not given to wine, no striker, not greedy of filthy lucre; but patient, not a brawler, not covetous;

2 Timothy 3:1-5 This know also, that in the last days perilous times shall come. 2 For men shall be lovers of their own selves, covetous, boasters, proud, blasphemers, disobedient to parents, unthankful, unholy, 3 Without natural affection, trucebreakers, false accusers, incontinent, fierce, despisers of those that are good, 4 Traitors, heady, highminded, lovers of pleasures more than lovers of God; 5 Having a form of godliness, but denying the power thereof: from such turn away.

Titus 2: 11-12 For the grace of God that bringeth salvation hath appeared to all men, 12 Teaching us that, denying ungodliness and worldly lusts, we should live soberly, righteously, and godly, in this present world;

2 Peter 1: 5-8 And beside this, giving all diligence, add to your faith virtue; and to virtue knowledge; 6 And to knowledge temperance; and to temperance patience; and to patience godliness; 7 And to godliness brotherly kindness; and to brotherly kindness charity. 8 For if these things be in you, and abound, they make you that ye shall neither be barren nor unfruitful in the knowledge of our Lord Jesus Christ.

2 Timothy 1:7 For God hath not given us the spirit of fear; but of power, and of love, and of a sound mind.

1 Corinthians 10:13 There hath no temptation taken you but such as is common to man: but God is faithful, who will not suffer you to be tempted above that ye are able; but will with the temptation also make a way to escape, that ye may be able to bear it.

Romans 12 :1 I beseech you therefore, brethren, by the mercies of God, that ye present your bodies a living sacrifice, holy, acceptable unto God, which is your reasonable service.

James 1:19-20 Wherefore, my beloved brethren, let every man be swift to hear, slow to speak, slow to wrath: 20 For the wrath of man worketh not the righteousness of God.

1 Corinthians 9: 24-25 Know ye not that they which run in a race run all, but one receiveth the prize? So run, that ye may obtain. 25 And every man that striveth for the mastery is temperate in all things. Now they do it to obtain a corruptible crown; but we an incorruptible.

1 Corinthians 6:12 All things are lawful unto me, but all things are not expedient: all things are lawful for me, but I will not be brought under the power of any.

2 Corinthians 12:9 And he said unto me, My grace is sufficient for thee: for my strength is made perfect in weakness. Most gladly therefore will I rather glory in my infirmities, that the power of Christ may rest upon me.

Make it
PERSONAL

On a scale of 1-10, with ten being the highest, rate your level of self-control in your life. Then rate the areas that are a struggle and compare the results.

1. What, if anything, needs to change?

2. Is every area of your life subject to self-control or are there some off-limits areas that need to be addressed?

Reference

https://en.wikipedia.org/wiki/Deliverance_ministry

~ The Author ~

Karen Hymon is the proud mother of three; two beautiful daughters and one amazing son, two wonderful sons in love and one spectacular daughter in love.

She has twelve inspiring and adorable grandchildren.

She is a veteran teacher of seventeen years, primarily for grades K-1, but has recently begun teaching children with special needs.

She is an ordained minister and is active in ministry at her church.

Karen Hymon is available for speaking and teaching engagements. You can connect with her via email at karenhymon@gmail.com

www.ingramcontent.com/pod-product-compliance
Lightning Source LLC
Chambersburg PA
CBHW071209160426
43196CB00011B/2235